NUREG–1280
Rev. 1

I0455445

Standard Format and Content Acceptance Criteria for the Material Control and Accounting (MC&A) Reform Amendment

10 CFR Part 74
Subpart E

Manuscript Completed: March 1995
Date Published: April 1995

Division of Fuel Cycle Safety and Safeguards
Office of Nuclear Material Safety and Safeguards
U.S. Nuclear Regulatory Commission
Washington, DC 20555–0001

ABSTRACT

In 1987 the NRC revised the material control and accounting requirements for NRC licensees authorized to possess and use a formula quantity (i.e., 5 formula kilograms or more) of strategic special nuclear material. Those revisions issued as 10 CFR 74.51-59 require timely monitoring of in-process inventory and discrete items to detect anomalies potentially indicative of material losses. Timely detection and enhanced loss localization capabilities are beneficial to alarm resolution and also for material recovery in the event of an actual loss. NUREG-1280 was issued in 1987 to present criteria that could be used by applicants, licensees, and NRC license reviewers in the initial preparation and subsequent review of fundamental nuclear material control (FNMC) plans submitted in response to the Reform Amendment. This document is also intended for both licensees and license reviewers with respect to FNMC plan revisions. General performance objectives, system capabilities, process monitoring, item monitoring, alarm resolution, quality assurance, and accounting are addressed. This revision to NUREG-1280 is an expansion of the initial edition, which clarifies and expands upon several topics and addresses issues identified under Reform Amendment implementation experience.

TABLE OF CONTENTS

TABLES

ACKNOWLEDGMENT

The NRC wishes to acknowledge the valuable technical contributions to this document from Pacific Northwest Laboratory (PNL), Richland, Washington, under contract to NRC. Principal contributors from PNL were: R. J. Brouns, L. C. Davenport, J. A. Piatt, F. P. Roberts, and B.W. Smith. Additionally, it should be noted that D. R. Joy (NRC, Division of Fuel Cycle Safety and Safeguards) provided considerable input for the Revision 1 edition of this NUREG.

ACRONYMS

AEC	Atomic Energy Commission
ANSI	American National Standards Institute
CAA	controlled access area
CFR	Code of Federal Regulations
CUMSRD	cumulative shipper-receiver difference
FKG	formula kilogram
FNMC	fundamental nuclear material control
HEU	high enriched uranium
ID	inventory difference
JPA	job performance aid
LEID	limit of error of the inventory difference
MAA	material access area
MBA	material balance area
MC&A	material control and accounting
NRC	Nuclear Regulatory Commission
NDA	nondestructive assay
PD	process difference
R&D	research and development
SEID	standard error of the inventory difference
SNM	special nuclear material
SRD	shipper-receiver difference
SSNM	strategic special nuclear material

INTRODUCTION

The Atomic Energy Act of 1954, as amended, directed the Atomic Energy Commission (AEC) to regulate the receipt, manufacture, production, transfer, possession, use, import, and export of special nuclear material (SNM) in order to protect the public health and safety, and to provide for the common defense and security. The Energy Reorganization Act of 1974 transferred all the licensing and related functions of the AEC to the Nuclear Regulatory Commission (NRC).

The principal requirements with respect to SNM licensing are found in Title 10, Code of Federal Regulations, Part 70 (10 CFR Part 70), "Special Nuclear Material" and Part 74 (10 CFR Part 74), "Material Control and Accounting of Special Nuclear Material." Paragraph (b) of §70.22 of 10 CFR Part 70 specifies that special nuclear material control and accounting (MC&A) information must be provided in a license application to show how compliance with the fundamental nuclear material control requirements of §70.58, §74.31, §74.33 or §74.51 will be accomplished.

Purpose and Applicability	This document describes the standard format and content suggested by the NRC for use in preparing fundamental nuclear material control (FNMC) plans in response to the Material Control and Accounting Reform Amendment (10 CFR 74.51). An intent and scope statement is provided for each requirement. These statements are intended to communicate the underlying objectives of each requirement and are not subject to negotiation in individual licensing actions. The document also provides acceptance criteria that will be used in evaluating the adequacy of submitted plans. To the extent possible, the criteria are presented in a performance-oriented format. Where prescriptive criteria were necessary, at least two alternatives normally are provided. Licensees are encouraged to develop additional alternative approaches, which provide an equivalent level of performance.
Use of the Standard Format	By using this standard format for preparing an FNMC plan, a license applicant will minimize administrative problems associated with the submittal, review, and approval of the plan. Preparation of an FNMC plan in accordance with this standard format will assist the NRC in evaluating the plan and in standardizing the licensing and review process. However, conformance with the standard format is not required by the NRC. An applicant may use a different format if it provides an equal level of completeness and detail.
	Regardless of the format, the applicant should employ a plan/annex concept. All fundamental commitments that define the bounds within which the licensee will function and the detailed level of the performance of its MC&A system should be included in the body of the plan. In those cases where a demonstration of a specific capability is called for, such information should be included in an annex to the plan which will not be incorporated as a condition of license. Procedures detailed in the annex may be

1

changed without NRC approval or notification provided plan commitments and capabilities are not degraded.

Statement of Affirmation
•

For completeness, the FMNC Plan should contain basic commitments called affirmations and a discussion of how these commitments will be achieved.

Use of Acceptance Criteria

The acceptance criteria are for the use of applicants (or licensees) and licensing reviewers. An application which meets these criteria should be acceptable to the NRC staff. However, as noted above, prescriptive criteria are included as examples, and each applicant should develop a MC&A program that takes into account the unique features of its particular operation.

Where additional guidance is available on particular topics, an appropriate reference is included in the acceptance criteria section.

Although this document is aimed at applicants for license, who must develop an FNMC plan from scratch, the guidance herein should also be utilized by licensees when making changes to their existing FNMC plan.

General Discussion

In this section, the license applicant should provide a general description of how its MC&A program satisfies the general performance objectives of paragraph 74.51(a). The description should include information on the plant, the process, and key features of the MC&A program including physical organization, types of tests, and classification of material as bulk versus items.

The description should be sufficiently general to allow for significant modification without necessitating revision of this section.

Questions and Answers:

Q Previously, the MC&A regulations of 10 CFR 70.51(e), 70.57, 70.58 applied to fuel facility licensees authorized to possess and use a quantity of special nuclear material (SNM) exceeding 1 effective kilogram. The MC&A Reform Amendments would apply to fuel facility licensees possessing and using 5 or more formula kilograms of strategic SNM (SSNM). What is the difference between effective and formula kilograms?

A 5 formula kilograms (FKG) of high-enriched uranium (HEU), plutonium, or 233-uranium has been established by the Commission as the quantity of strategic importance. For plutonium or 233-uranium, the number of formula kilograms

2

is defined as 2.5 times the weight in kilograms of the plutonium or 233-uranium. For HEU enriched to 20% or more in 235-uranium, it is defined as the weight in kilograms of the 235-uranium isotope. For plutonium or 233-uranium, an effective kilogram is defined as the weight in kilograms of the plutonium or 233-uranium. For uranium enriched in the 235-uranium isotope more than 1% (0.01 weight fraction), it is defined as the weight in kilograms of the uranium element multiplied by the square of its enrichment expressed as a decimal weight fraction.

The Reform Amendments apply to HEU, plutonium, and 233-uranium in quantities of 5 FKG or more. For plutonium and 233-uranium, 5 FKG is the same amount of material as 2 effective kilograms. For HEU, 5 FKG varies from 1 effective kilogram for 20% enrichment to 5 effective kilograms for 100% enrichment. Licensees possessing and using more than 1 effective kilogram of SNM of moderate strategic significance continue to be subject to the requirements of 10 CFR 70.51, 70.57, and 70.58. Licensees possessing and using more than 1 effective kilogram of SNM of low strategic significance would be subject to the requirements of 10 CFR 74.31, or in the case of uranium enrichment facilities to 10 CFR 74.33.

Threat Definition [§74.51(b)]

Questions and Answers:

Q Why is the collusion protection requirement different from that in 10 CFR 73.1(a)?

A The physical protection requirements of 10 CFR 73.1(a) stipulate that collusion protection be provided against the conspiracy detailed in the design basis threat. To require the MC&A system to also protect against the same conspiracy would be excessive. The provisions of the MC&A Reform Amendments are designed to function in an integrated fashion with those of 10 CFR Part 73 while adding an independent verification, thus producing a more cost-effective system. Under this new approach, MC&A is only required to protect against an insider's ability to cover up his/her theft.

The MC&A system needs to protect against only a single insider, providing that individual does not have authority within the physical protection system that would permit him/her to participate in a conspiracy aimed at defeating the safeguards system. If an MC&A individual does have authority within the physical protection system, then the MC&A system is required to protect against the cover-up of a collusion of that individual with any other individual having MC&A authority.

This approach should relieve licensees of most of the burden that would result from requiring a totally redundant system while still maintaining the ability of the MC&A system to provide an extra level of independent protection and an added measure of assurance that the safeguards system as a whole has not been compromised.

Q   What are examples of things this collusion requirement would affect?

A   Under this provision, the licensee is required to analyze all positions having responsibility within the MC&A system to determine if any also have responsibility within the physical protection system. A safeguards manager might be an example of such a position. If this position includes both MC&A and physical protection responsibilities, procedures would have to be developed to ensure that when an individual in this job is performing an MC&A function, that this function be performed under a three-person rule, be independently checked later by a third party, or be otherwise protected against abuse of authority.

For some individuals in management/supervisory positions, some modifications to procedures, such as restricted access without escort to some areas, may be necessary to provide sufficient assurance that the system cannot be compromised.

An MC&A function performed by a worker without physical protection system authority would need to be protected against a single insider threat. However, it would need no cross-check if that individual had no "hands on" access to formula quantities of SSNM (e.g., a laboratory chemist).

1.0 ABRUPT LOSS DETECTION

1.1 Unit Process Detection Capability

Requirement

The rule requires that for each unit process, a licensee establish a production quality control program capable of monitoring the status of material in-process. The program should include material control tests; the results of which would be subjected to the following:

- A statistical test that has at least a 95% power of detecting an abrupt loss of 5 formula kilograms within 3 working days of a loss of Category IA material from any accessible process location and 7 calendar days of a loss of Category IB material from any accessible process location [§74.53(b)(1)],

- A quality control test whereby results greater than both three times the estimated standard deviation of the process difference estimator and 25 grams of SSNM are investigated [§74.53(b)(2)], and

- A trend analysis for monitoring and evaluating sequences of material control test results from each unit process to determine if they indicate a statistically significant recurrent loss or gain [§74.53(b)(3)].

Intent and Scope

The intent of these requirements is to have a quality control program that will provide early indications of diversion or theft and a prompt detection system for significant abrupt diversions of 5 FKG or more. Through prompt detection, response and recovery actions can be initiated soon after a loss event while circumstances surrounding the loss occurrence are fresh in the minds of cognizant personnel, and materials are available for remeasurement. In addition, fewer changes in process conditions, inventories, in-process holdups, and item locations will have occurred so that resolution probabilities are enhanced. The detection times for a 5 FKG loss are maximums; hence, a licensee may use shorter intervals for specific unit processes if so desired.

1.1.1 Process Subdivision and Measurement Points

Describe the subdivision of the process to meet the unit detection requirements and the associated parameters to be measured and the measurement points. A diagram or listing may be used to document this information.

Affirmation:

The process is subdivided to satisfy test criteria for the category of material being processed.

Acceptance Criteria:

All SSNM in bulk form in the material access area (MAA) is within the span of a material control test. [Note: Exceptions to this requirement include (1) low-level waste that meets the criteria in 10 CFR 73.46(c)(6), (2) laboratory samples each containing less than 0.05 FKG, (3) SSNM in research and development operations with throughputs of less than 5 FKG during any 7 consecutive days, and (4) SSNM in waste treatment operations conducted outside an MAA, (e.g., incinerator).]

There is no limit or restriction on the number of control units into which a facility can be divided. Loss detection sensitivity, false alarm rate, and loss localization capability are key determining factors. The following criteria are appropriate in determining control unit boundaries:

- Material control tests should be performed on units generally consistent with readily assessable measurement points which naturally result from the process design. Process units should not be divided into smaller units for material control tests if such subdivision would cause the standard deviation of the test statistic to increase from below 850 formula grams 235-uranium (or equivalent units for tests not based on 235-uranium) to above 850 formula grams 235-uranium unless such subdivision is necessary to meet the timeliness criteria of §74.53(b)(1).

- Batch transfers should be used wherever they occur.

- Process variabilities should be localized to a control unit.

- Concentration differences between feed and product stream output should be minimized wherever possible.

- Process units that operate continuously should be separated (in terms of defining control unit test boundaries) from those that operate in a batch mode.

- False alarm rates should be minimized. The number of false alarms per inventory period should be less than 1% of all tests.

1.1.2 Material Control Tests

Describe the material control tests for each unit process. The description should include:

1) Identification of the test statistic,
2) The amounts and types of data used to establish uncertainties (sigmas),
3) Tests for normality,
4) Means of handling non-normal data,

5) Tests for outliers,
6) Methods for establishing alarm thresholds,
7) Criteria for modifying alarm thresholds, and
8) The basis for assignment of the start times for each material control test.

In the Annex provide:

1) A detailed example alarm threshold calculation for a process unit,
2) A tabulation of the threshold values for all process units,
3) A tabulation of the detection times associated with each material control test,
4) The justification for the derivation of each threshold value, and
5) A listing of category IA and IB materials and the justification for the lower classification of the latter.

Affirmations: Material control anomalies resulting from material control tests will be investigated when such anomalies exceed 3 times the standard deviation of the test statistic and 25 grams of SSNM. Results are documented.

The detection system is capable of detecting a 5 FKG (or more) abrupt loss of Category IA material within 3 working days and Category IB material within 7 calendar days of the loss occurrence from any accessible location within a unit process.

The action thresholds for the material control tests are updated, at least annually, based on the previous 6 months of operating data and as supported by the analysis of test data.

Automated or manual records of the location, movement, quantity, and identity of SSNM are maintained as needed to perform the material control tests for abrupt loss detection.

Acceptance Criteria: The licensee has developed a system of material control tests for detecting abrupt losses of bulk material from single units or locations within the facility. The material control tests are capable of detecting a 5 FKG loss with at least 95% probability of detection. The material control tests have the following characteristics:

• Each material control test encompasses the SSNM in a definite unit or location or over a span of locations comprising a segment of the process or a single point in the process.

- The material control test is based on a comparison of a measured value(s) of a quantity of material(s) or of a process variable with a reference value. The reference value is the expected or predicted quantity of material or value of the process variable in the absence of diversion or unexpected loss. Examples of possible material control tests are:

    - SSNM material balance,

    - Mass (weight) balance,

    - Volume balance,

    - Yield versus expected or predicted yield,

    - Liquid level versus predicted level,

    - Solution density versus predicted density,

    - Flow rate versus predicted flow rate,

    - Bulk powder volume or volume times bulk density versus predicted quantity,

    - Nondestructive assay (NDA) value versus predicted value,

    - Isotopic ratio versus predicted value,

    - Number of units, such as pellets, elements, or pins, versus predicted number, and

    - Process control parameters, such as pH, reagent volume, or extraction efficiency, versus predicted values.

- Each material control test has an action threshold (critical value) which, if exceeded, initiates the alarm resolution procedures prescribed in §74.57. In general, the action threshold or critical value can be set by a formula of the following type:

$A = +G + \bar{x} - K\sigma_x$ (when x increases upon real loss), or

$A = -G + \bar{x} + K\sigma_x$ (when x decreases upon real loss)

where: A = alarm threshold in terms of test value obtained for x (as formula grams SSNM)

G = goal quantity = 5000 formula grams or less

x = test statistic (parameter) such as feed input minus product output for a given test period, as formula grams SSNM

$\bar{x}$ = test statistic mean, assuming the null hypothesis, H_o, is true (H_o: L=0), as formula grams SSNM [Note: This mean value can be either positive or negative]

L = loss quantity

K = factor based on Probability of Detection

σ_x = standard deviation of the test statistics, as formula grams SSNM

Key considerations applicable to this determination are:

1) If the distribution of the source data can be reasonably represented by a single normal model after the effects of human errors have been eliminated, use K=1.65 to achieve 95% detection probability.

2) If an analysis of test data indicates the presence of multiple distributions, one of the following actions would be appropriate:

   Undertake an in-depth study to identify the sources of error and the adjustments that should be made, as appropriate, so that a single normal distribution adequately represents the data.

   or

   Estimate the parameters ($\bar{x}, \sigma_x$) using a computer program as necessary, to maximize the likelihood function; then the critical point is determined by integrating the probability density function to the probability of interest.

   or

   Determine whether the presence of multiple distributions is the result of concomitant data which occurred as the result of some recognized change that occurred during the test period (e.g., new and recycled material processed through an operation). If such data are available, the data should be split into subsets for testing.

3) If a non-zero $\bar{x}$ is used, a study should be conducted to identify the cause(s). The chosen $\bar{x}$ should minimize the σ_x for the test statistic.

- When data do not seem to fit a normal distribution, an evaluation should be made to see if some mathematical function of the data values will fit (transformation of data). A commonly used transformation is logarithms, which is the basis for the lognormal distribution.

- Although there is no stated limit on the magnitude of the measurement and/or process uncertainty, the establishment of alarm thresholds indirectly limits magnitude of these errors. That is, when the standard deviation of the test statistic becomes a large fraction of "G," there is an excessive number of false alarms.

- The combined quality of the material control test and loss resolution decisions shall permit alarms remaining unresolved after the completion of investigative activities to be good indicators of an actual loss. To achieve this objective, the licensee should demonstrate that the statistically expected number of unresolved false alarms will be less than 0.10 per inventory period for all abrupt bulk loss alarms exceeding 5 FKG (i.e., the predicted number of such unresolved alarms should be less than 1 in 10 inventory periods).

- The action thresholds are based on statistical hypothesis tests derived from the variances of the test statistics or on other technical bases for which it can be shown that the power of the test for loss is satisfactory.

- The measurement variances assumed by the licensee are either supported by published typical values [see Reilly and Evans (1977), Rodgers (1982), or Reilly et al. (1991)], the licensee's measurement control data, or historical data from the licensee's process or other similar processes. The assumed process variances may be estimated by using conservative judgments based on sound engineering principles if historical performance data for the licensee's process or similar processes are not available. If engineering judgments or typical values are used, the Plan should include provisions and schedules for updating the estimated variances with actual performance data. The methods of estimating the loss detection sensitivity or the variances of loss detection parameters are satisfactorily explained and a credible justification for their use is given.

10

The tests for detecting abrupt losses at each accessible location meet the 3 and 7 day detection time goals for Category IA and Category IB materials, respectively, under all routine conditions that are expected to prevail at the location. (Note: When detection times are interrupted by idle time caused by such things as weekends, holidays or vacations, the licensee has provisions for completing the tests before the idle time or for conducting additional tests to cover any material control tests that will not be completed. The additional tests achieve the same level of detection as the principal tests.)

The licensee's classification of the process material as Category IA and Category IB is explained and justified in the Annex. Category IB materials must be at least one of the following:

1) Not usable for constructing a nuclear explosive device without further processing,

2) Not susceptible to undetected removal from the MAA by an insider because of size, weight, or chemical hazard, or

3) Of such low concentrations of SSNM that excessively large bulk quantities would be needed to obtain a formula quantity of SSNM.

The timeliness of abrupt loss detection at a single location is based on the interval between the time a goal quantity of SSNM becomes accessible for diversion and the completion of the material control test. The start time occurs when the quantity of SSNM is first equal to or greater than the established goal quantity.

Process difference estimates that exceed both 3 times the standard deviation of their estimator and 25 grams of SSNM must be investigated and the results documented. The investigation should as a minimum include:

• A review of all source data and calculations for errors,

• A review of material control test results for the preceding SSNM quantity in the involved unit and the results of material control tests from the two adjacent units,

• An interview with process operators to ascertain if a perturbation in the process may have occurred,

• A check of sidestreams for abnormally high SSNM content,

- An assessment of the possibility that additional holdup beyond what had been projected may have occurred, and

- When necessary, a check of safety and backup systems common to several (or all) process units, such as ventilation filters and scrubbers, effluent monitors, etc., for indications of abnormally high process losses.

Questions and Answers:

Q What forms of SSNM are covered by this section?

A Bulk materials, including nontamper-safed containers of SSNM (not within a vault or permanently CAA), as well as materials in process equipment, are covered. In general, these requirements apply to material that has to be measured to verify its presence, rather than have its identification number and seal or encapsulation integrity checked.

Q Are licensees required to detect process related losses of amounts smaller than 5 FKG?

A The Commission has judged the risk to the public's health and safety of losses of less than 5 FKG of SSNM to be relatively small compared to losses of more than that amount. Under previous MC&A regulations, which included limits that were proportional to plant throughput, a small throughput licensee was required to keep inventory differences less than a few hundred grams, while a large throughput facility was allowed to operate with inventory differences of more than 5 FKG. The MC&A Reform Amendment applies the same detection goal quantity to all category I licensees, both large and small. § 74.53 requires the detection of single process related abrupt losses of 5 FKG (or more) with 95% or greater probability. Such a system will also provide a capability to detect smaller losses with reduced detection probability.

Furthermore, each licensee who possesses 1 gram or more of 235-uranium, 233-uranium, or plutonium is required by 10 CFR 74.11 to report any actual known loss of SSNM, regardless of quantity.

Q Is it necessary to close a material balance to achieve the detection capabilities?

A In contrast to previous regulations, it is not the intent of the Reform Amendment to require measured balances as the only acceptable material control test for detection of losses.

It is the intent of the Reform Amendment to ensure that the detection and localization performance criteria of the rule are met. In some cases, a licensee may find no satisfactory alternative to closing a material balance in order to satisfy the performance criteria. In other cases, alternatives will be feasible. (For example, see pages 4-8 of NUREG/CR-1670, Volume 1, "The Use of Process Monitoring Data for Nuclear Material Accounting," October 1980, and pages 12-13 of NUREG/CR-1686, Volume 1, "Feasibility and Cost/Benefit of Advanced Safeguards for Control of Nuclear Material In-Process," October 1980.)

Q The measurement system error is not constrained by the detection probability requirement without a false alarm limit. Isn't there a limit on how big the measurement error can be?

A The problem that comes from too large a measurement or process uncertainty, which causes the standard deviation of the test statistic to be a large fraction of the goal quantity, is excessive false alarms. The rule does not limit the number of false alarms allowed. However, the alarm resolution requirements must be met. One approach to meeting those requirements is to reduce expected false alarms to a level below the acceptable number of unresolvable alarms. Another approach is to tolerate a fairly high rate of false alarms and have more accurate backup measurement systems or more accurate downstream measurements to help resolve the false alarms. Criteria for the acceptability of the alarm resolution approach provide the limits on measurement error for detection and response.

Q Why is there a requirement to investigate process differences that exceed 3 times the standard deviation of their estimator and 25 grams of SSNM?

A Differences that exceed 3 standard deviations are expected to be good quality control indicators for anomalies that could have an adverse impact on MC&A. In some units, differences of such a magnitude might trigger an alarm potentially indicative of a 5 FKG loss, in which case alarm resolution procedures would be initiated. In other cases, the differences may be far less than the quantity necessary to trigger an alarm; however, investigative action is appropriate before the problem escalates to a more serious situation.

Q What constitutes a "working day" as used in this part?

A A working day is any 24-hour calendar day (from 12:01 AM to 12:00 midnight) during which material processing activities occur and there is material handling, except for those calendar days in which the only processing and material handling activities are limited to the first and/or last 30 minutes of the day, due to the ending or beginning of shift scheduling times. A day during which activities such as maintenance of equipment, cleanup, autoclave monitoring, etc., occur would not be considered a work day unless SSNM handling was involved. The main criteria are whether or not SSNM handling is involved, and whether or not the activities would afford the opportunity for diversion or theft.

1.1.3 Location Categorization

Identify the SSNM locations within the facility classified as inaccessible (relative to SSNM accessibility by a single individual).

In the annex provide the justification for classifying a location as inaccessible.

Affirmations:

All SSNM locations within the facility that are considered to be inaccessible will be identified and the supporting rationale provided.

Acceptance Criteria:

For the purpose of establishing the start time for material control tests, SSNM may be treated as not accessible for diversion if:

• Access to SSNM is physically precluded without the need for visible puncturing, breaking, or otherwise violating the integrity of the process equipment containing the SSNM; or

• The state of the SSNM precludes diversion because of high temperature, chemical reactivity, radioactivity, or other chemical or physical properties; or

• The removal of the SSNM from its authorized location cannot be accomplished because the tools or equipment needed for its movement are unavailable, or

• The SSNM is a large volume of dilute solution within a large vessel, the absence of which (i.e., the SSNM) could not escape notice; or

• The material is under continuous surveillance of two or more individuals or an electronic or other type of monitoring system that will detect attempts by a single individual to remove material from a process.

Questions and Answers:

Q Are losses from any location required to be detected, or only losses from accessible locations?

A   Losses from any location must be detected. The concept of accessible location applies only to the criteria for establishing and determining the timeliness of the licensees' detection capabilities. The detection time is the duration from when the SSNM passes a place from where it is accessible to diversion to the time at which its loss would be detected. Licensees are encouraged to have few accessible locations since the risk of material being stolen is reduced by minimizing opportunities for people to have access to material or to have access to points of remote control over material flow if those controls could be used to divert the flow into unauthorized locations.

Q   Should a glovebox be considered an "accessible location?"

A   Generally yes. Since such activities as a glove change or "bagging out" operation are considered routine, a removal of material via this route may not be readily detectable. However, if there is an enforceable policy that all removals from a glovebox must be accomplished by at least two individuals and there are no access points which could be accessed without an obvious indication, a glovebox may be treated as inaccessible.

1.1.4 Material Substitution

Identify all credible substitute materials (for both simple and isotopic substitution) at each location and the method of testing for substitution or of controlling the substitute material to prevent or detect attempts at substitution. The method of preventing credible substitute materials from being covertly introduced should also be described. (NOTE: Reference to the Physical Protection Plan is permitted.)

Affirmations: Where credible substitute material is present and not controlled, the material control tests are capable of detecting diversions or thefts involving substitution of other material(s) for SSNM.

or

No credible substitute materials are permitted inside the MAA, nor is it credible that substitute materials could be covertly introduced from outside the MAA.

or

Credible substitute materials are available within the MAA; however, sufficient controls are in place to preclude their use to conceal diversion.

15

Acceptance Criteria: The material control tests need only detect those losses not involving substitution unless credible materials are available in the same MAA in the form of uncontrolled material or are not prohibited as contraband from being brought into the MAA.

Where credible substitute material is present and uncontrolled, the material control tests must be capable of detecting diversions employing substitution with the loss sensitivity and probability of detection required in §74.53. If uranium of a lower enrichment is a credible uncontrolled substitute, a material control test must be capable of detecting isotopic dilution. Otherwise, a test that detects replacement of plutonium or uranium SSNM by another element is adequate.

Material is deemed not to be a credible substitute if it satisfies any of the following:

• Has physical properties such as density, color, particle size, or other characteristics that will be immediately and unequivocally recognized to be different from the SSNM by personnel who routinely work with the SSNM;

• Has chemical properties that will always cause process upsets or degradation of product quality severe enough to be recognized and reported to a designated individual responsible to initiating a response within the time period of the material control test;

• Is controlled by a monitoring technique and/or physical controls that prevent its substitution for SSNM; or

• Is controlled by a material accounting test that will detect losses or diversion of the substitute material and in the absence of an alarm will provide indirect assurance that an SSNM diversion involving substitution has not occurred.

Acceptable controls on substitute materials might include the following:

• Access to the material is controlled through isolation in a locked limited access cabinet or room and access is restricted to individuals who would not be involved in the actual handling of SSNM during production operations;

• Periodic material balances are performed on the substitute material inventory where the balance may merely entail a weight comparison of material on starting inventory plus additions to inventory minus material issued for production vs. the current inventory weight;

- Semi-quantitative NDA tests are performed on intermediate product materials from process operations where credible substitute materials might be introduced; or

- Credible substitute materials are stored outside the MAA and introduced only in amounts for a shift or day's production.

1.1.5 Exemptions

Provide a listing of material types exempted from the abrupt loss detection tests with their locations and discuss the basis for the exemptions.

Affirmations:

All materials not qualifying for exemption under §74.53(a)(1), (2), (3), or (4) are included under a material control test.

Acceptance Criteria:

For low throughput operations such as waste compactors and incinerators where throughput is less than 5 FKG in 3 months and the measurement uncertainties (at the 2 σ level) on inputs and/or outputs are greater than 10%, the licensee performs material balances on a batch basis and makes appropriate corrections to the originating unit(s) or area cumulative balances to the extent practicable. Holdup determinations are necessary only at the time of the physical inventory (or sooner for criticality safety reasons), and input-output differences are assessed only to the extent that significant trends are investigated to identify measurement biases or an unaccounted for loss stream.

For samples containing greater than 0.05 FKG and scrap and waste containers in laboratories, the licensee performs monthly material balances. These balances may be accomplished by:

- Maintaining a dynamic record of the laboratory inventory,

- Maintaining a continuous inventory of the contents of scrap and waste containers by tracking the amounts of all additions (or removals) to each container, and

- Measuring the contents of each container monthly to detect significant discrepancies where "significant" is defined as more than 2 times the standard deviation of the difference estimator.

1.1.6 Trend Analysis

Describe the trend analysis techniques that are employed to monitor sequences of process differences from material control tests. The description should include the decision criteria for ascertaining when a significant trend exists.

Affirmations:

Procedures are implemented and maintained for monitoring and evaluating sequences of loss or gain estimates for each unit process, and anomalous trends in sequences of abrupt loss

17

estimators are tested to determine if they indicate a pattern of recurrent losses or gains that are of safeguards significance.

Acceptance Criteria: The trend analysis required by §74.53(b)(3) can be accomplished by the application of appropriate parametric or nonparametric statistical techniques. Examples include: Page's Test, Runs Test, Dietz's Test, Power One Test, and a MOSUM Test (e.g., Picard 1986 or Johnston 1987).

With respect to "safeguards significance" as it pertains to trend analysis, a trend should be considered significant when the applied test indicates it to be so and the absolute quantity involved is in excess of 3 FKG.

To select a trend analysis test, historical data should be evaluated to determine whether the assumptions of the statistical test are appropriate, including distribution of data and independence of successive data.

Two process difference estimates in succession within the same process control unit that exceed 3 times the standard deviation of their estimators and their sum exceeds 3 FKG, where both suggest a loss or a gain, should trigger additional investigative measures that include:

• Notification of the nuclear materials control manager,

• Review of security records,

• Added surveillance measures in the involved process unit, and

• Conducting a physical inventory of the associated MBA within 2 months.

Questions and Answers: Q What is to be accomplished by a trend analysis?

A Non-random behavior of process differences may indicate the presence of an unidentified bias, unmeasured loss stream, or a diversion. It is important that trends be identified so that investigations can be initiated to uncover the cause.

1.2 Research and Development Operations   [§74.53(c)(1) & (2)]

Requirements   For research and development operations, the rule requires each licensee to:

1) Perform material balance tests on a lot or batch basis, as appropriate, or monthly, whichever is sooner, and investigate any difference greater than 200 grams of plutonium or 233-uranium or 300 grams of 235-uranium and which also exceeds 3 times the standard error of the ID estimator; and

2) Evaluate material balance results generated during an inventory period for indications of bias or unidentified loss streams and investigate cumulative differences greater than 3 FKG of SSNM.

Intent and Scope

By design, R&D operations are dynamic in nature. Thus, the prompt loss detection techniques that depend upon process yields are inappropriate for loss detection. Taking into account the low throughput of such operations, periodic material balance tests on a batch or monthly are deemed acceptable for loss detection.

1.2.1 Lot/Batch Characterization

Provide the criteria that are used to define a lot or batch.

Affirmations:

Material balance tests are performed on lots or batches of material from R&D operations or on a monthly basis, whichever is sooner.

Acceptance Criteria:

Proposed materials groupings into lots or batches are acceptable taking into account prompt loss detection objectives, measurement characterization, and processing constraints.

1.2.2 Material Balance Tests

Describe how the components of a process material balance are established including the degree to which a process will be cleaned out and/or holdup measurements will be performed. Discuss the handling of scrap including measurement, pre-treatment prior to recovery, and segregation.

Affirmations:

Inventory differences that exceed 300 grams of 235-uranium (or 200 grams plutonium or 233-uranium) and 3 times the standard error of the ID estimator are investigated and resolved.

Sequences of inventory differences are monitored for indications of a trend and cumulative differences (occurring within an inventory period) exceeding 3 FKG are investigated.

Acceptance Criteria:

For R&D material balances, the inputs to the standard error of the inventory difference are reasonable and include all sources of measurement error.

Inventory differences on R&D lots or batches generated during an inventory period may be based on weight comparisons provided:

• The lots or batches represent intermediate products,

- The input materials to the R&D facility are measured for element and/or isotope,

- There are no credible substitute materials present in the MAA or adequate controls exist to preclude the use of substitute materials to conceal a diversion,

- The quantity of SSNM in sidestreams can be reliably measured, and

- The ultimate product of the operation is measured for element and/or isotope, as appropriate.

2.0 ITEM MONITORING

2.1 Item Loss Detection

Requirement

The rule requires that each licensee establish the capability to detect a 5 FKG or greater loss in item form using any statistical test that has a 99% power of detection. Detection is to occur within:

1) 30 calendar days of a Category IA loss and 60 calendar days of a Category IB loss for those items in a vault or permanently controlled access area (CAA) isolated from the rest of the MAA [§74.55(b)(1)],

2) 3 working days of a Category IA loss and 7 calendar days of a Category IB loss for items located elsewhere in the MAA except that a 5 FKG or greater loss of encapsulated SSNM components that are each at least 1 meter in length and in excess of 30 kilograms is to be detected within 30 calendar days [§74.55(b)(2)],

3) 60 calendar days for the loss of Category IB items of waste stored in a permanently CAA outside of an MAA [§74.55(b)(3)], and

4) 60 calendar days for samples in a vault or permanently CAA and 30 calendar days for samples elsewhere in the MAA for those samples each containing less than 0.05 FKG of SSNM [§74.55(b)(4)].

Pursuant to §74.55(a), items, except samples, are to be uniquely identified, quantitatively measured, with the validity of the measurement independently confirmed. Additionally, items are to be either:

1) Tamper-safed or placed in a vault or permanently CAA that provides protection at least equivalent to tamper-safing, or

2) Sealed such that removal of SSNM would be readily and permanently apparent (e.g., encapsulated).

Intent and Scope

The intent of this requirement is to ensure timely plant-wide detection of the loss of items that total 5 FKG or more. To achieve this capability, the licensee is expected to verify the presence and integrity of selected SSNM items on a periodic basis. The required frequency of tests for missing items is graded according to the relative attractiveness of the material type in the item, the ease with which the item could be diverted without

21

being observed, and the degree of surveillance and containment provided for by the material control and physical security systems. SSNM is not to be considered as being in item form unless it falls into at least one of the following categories:

(1) it is encapsulated,

(2) it is within a tamper-safe sealed container,

(3) it is stored within a vault,

(4) it is stored in a permanently CAA that provides protection at least equivalent to tamper-safing, or

(5) it is contained in samples each containing less than 0.05 FKG.

If SSNM is not in item form, as defined above, it must be subjected to the in-process control requirements for bulk material unless it qualifies for exemption under §74.53(a)(2), (3) or (4).

The longer detection times for losses of items from permanently CAAs take into account the added security afforded by the physical protection measures required of such areas by 10 CFR Part 73. However, this provision should not be interpreted as authorizing the placement of materials in these areas other than those already authorized pursuant to Part 73.

2.1.1 Item Identification

Describe the identification system (numeric or alpha-numeric) used to assign a unique identification to each item. The description should include the features of the system that preclude falsification or that ensure prompt detection of such attempts.

Affirmations:

Each SSNM item is uniquely identified; the SSNM content is quantitatively measured; the validity of the measurement is independently confirmed and ensured through encapsulation, tamper-safing, or storage in a vault or permanently CAA that provides protection at least equivalent to tamper-safing; and a record of the identity, location, date of creation, SSNM content, and utilized measurement method is maintained.

Acceptance Criteria:

The item identification system possesses attributes that ensure unique item identification, preclude falsification, or as a minimum, make prompt detection of such attempts highly probable. Factors to be considered in achieving this objective are:

- The use of tamper-safe seal numbers for unique identification represents an attractive alternative because: the same number is used for both seal and item tracking, seal numbers cannot

be altered without leaving visible evidence, and seal
distribution and usage are controlled;

- The use of prenumbered containers which retain the same
  identification for repeat uses should generally be avoided
  unless detailed usage records are maintained that reflect the
  source and disposition of items including times to fractions of
  a day; and

- The use of preprinted labels or blank labels that are numbered
  as they are used is acceptable provided unauthorized alteration
  or replacement of the labels would be readily apparent to a
  knowledgeable observer.

2.1.2 Item Classification

Provide the basis for classifying items as material Category IB
and any proposed exemptions from item control tests or from
response actions, including a listing of the item categories
involved and the rationale for such exemptions.

Affirmations:

Items are classified as either Category IA or IB at the time they
are created in order to fix the frequency of tests for item loss.

Acceptance Criteria:

The methods used to classify items are consistent with those
defined in Section 1.1.2 (*Material Control Tests*) for process
monitoring. The record system shows whether an item has been
classified as IA or IB.

2.1.3 Tamper-safing

Describe the tamper-safing procedures employed to ensure the
continuing validity of previously measured and attested to SSNM
values assigned to unique items.

Aspects to be addressed include: personnel involvement, types of
seals, attesting to declarations, records, and inspection methods
for detecting violations of item integrity.

Affirmations:

Only tamper-indicating devices which are controlled and
accounted for are used to maintain the validity of previously
established SSNM quantities associated with items.

Acceptance Criteria:

The acceptability of tamper-seals is based on an evaluation of the
seal attributes in relation to time to defeat and tamper-indicating
features. Seals already deemed acceptable by NRC include:
Type E, Pressure-sensitive, and Steel Padlock. Other seals, such
as fiber optic, may be equally acceptable. The licensee must
provide the appropriate information, including references, to
enable licensing reviewers to assess the adequacy of other than
currently approved seals.

The control of seals and seal records precludes or makes readily apparent any attempts at illicit use of seals. Potential contributors to these objectives include commitments that:

- Seals are stored in a locked repository within a room that is locked when unoccupied,

- Blocks of seals issued to designated individuals are afforded the same level of protection,

- Preferably a single individual, but no more than three individuals, none of whom have any responsibility for seal application or destruction, is (are) designated as the seal control officer(s),

- The seal log book maintained by the control officer(s) is kept separate from the seals and stored in a locked repository,

- Individuals responsible for applying seals either have unused seals in their personal possession or place them in a limited access locked compartment. As a rule, the number of available seals issued to these individuals should be limited to a single day's use,

- The licensee has in his possession a commitment from the seal manufacturer that plates and/or dies and production residuals are controlled and protected, and

- Used Type E seals are crimped, flattened, or otherwise rendered unusable and properly disposed of.

2.1.4 Accessibility

Describe the personnel access controls, the surveillance procedures, and the records procedures for entrance and exit of personnel to and from vaults and/or permanently CAAs. If any of the above attributes are described in sufficient detail in the facility's Physical Security Plan, appropriate references may be made.

Affirmations: Vaults or permanently CAAs that are subject to 30-day (IA) or 60-day (IB) test frequencies and isolated from the rest of the MAA are operated with physical and administrative controls over personnel access such that unauthorized additions and removals of items from the storage area will be either prevented or promptly detected.

Acceptance Criteria: Storage that meets the physical security requirements for vaults, documented in Part 73, will meet the requirements of 10 CFR 74.55 for storage of items containing either Category IA or IB material.

Storage that meets the following requirements will be accepted as a CAA, isolated from the rest of the MAA for the purposes of 10 CFR 74.55:

- CAA is constructed and/or equipped with physical protection capabilities that deter and detect unauthorized access,

- Access to the storage area is limited to the minimum number of persons necessary and records are kept of the persons who enter and leave it,

- Records of the items in storage are maintained, and

- An individual within the storage area is continuously observed by another person, and all additions, removals, and movements of material are verifiable by at least two individuals.

Storage provides protection at least equivalent to tamper-safing if:

- Access to the vault or CAA is limited to the minimum number of persons necessary, and records are kept of the persons who enter and leave it,

- The personnel authorized to enter and operate the vault or CAA are not authorized to remove or handle SSNM beyond the boundaries of the vault or area unless controls are in place that would preclude an individual from surreptitiously removing an item or any portion of an untamper-sealed container,

- At all times, a person within a vault or permanently CAA is accompanied by at least one other person and all activities by any person are verifiable by another. In addition, remote surveillance, such as closed circuit television, with the capability of seeing all operators at all times is used. The remote surveillance need not be continuous if the occupants cannot determine or predict when they may be under surveillance. However, the time of remote surveillance should, on the average, equal at least 25 percent of the non-surveillance time, and any interval of non-surveillance should not exceed 5 minutes.

- The SSNM content of nontamper-safed, and unencapsulated, items is measured, independently confirmed by a second person, and the item is under the continuous surveillance of the two persons from the time of measurement until placed in a vault or CAA,

- The SSNM contents of nontamper-safed, and unencapsulated, items are verified by quantitative measurements when removed from a vault or CAA except for solid components which can be verified by a weight check. The verification measurement is equivalent to (or better than) the original measurement in terms of measurement uncertainty. The verification measurement and the original result agree within the combined measurement uncertainties. (Note: Random errors will generally be the only component of the uncertainty except in those instances where a recalibration of the measurement process has taken place.) The verification measurement also detects substitution except where it can be demonstrated that no credible substitute material is present in the vault or CAA, and

- The response actions documented in Chapter 3.0 of the FNMC plan are initiated if an unauthorized vault or CAA penetration is known or suspected to have occurred, or if the SSNM content of any container is unexplainable and significantly different from the recorded value.

2.1.5 *Accounting and Control Procedures*

Describe the item accounting and control procedures for items placed in and removed from secure storage. The description should include item inventory records utilized.

Affirmations:

The operating procedures of item storage areas are documented.

Every change of inventory in the storage area is recorded.

A designated individual is responsible for the operation of each such storage area.

The response actions documented in Chapter 3.0 of the FNMC plan will be initiated if one or more items are missing except where the missing items total less than 50 grams 235-uranium, 233-uranium, or plutonium.

Acceptance Criteria:

Procedures approved by the Material Control and Accountability orgainzation, are utilized and reviewed annually for all secure storage areas.

Each procedure must designate the individual responsible for that secure storage area and describe the method and inventory records used for documenting additions or withdrawals of items from the area.

2.1.6 Item Measurements

Identify the measurement systems used to quantify the SSNM content of items at item creation time. The description also must include the confirmatory measurements used to quantitatively verify the SSNM content of nontamper-safed, and unencapsulated, items placed into or removed from vault storage or a CAA that is equivalent to tamper-safing, including the controls that prevent or detect attempts at substitution.

Affirmations:

Accountability and confirmatory measurement systems are identified and described in written procedures.

Acceptance Criteria:

Independent confirmation of the SSNM content of items will be achieved by having a second person do the following:

- Observe the bulk measurement and sampling of the item whose contents are to be determined, or

- Observe the nondestructive analysis of the item, or

- Perform a second quantitative analysis independently that does not destroy the integrity of the item,

and

- Witness and attest to the application of an approved tamper-seal, or

- Accompany the first person and the item to a vault or permanently CAA which will provide storage equivalent to tamper-safing.

2.1.7 Item Verification

Describe the item verification procedure. The description must include:

- The inventory sampling method, including the sample size selection equations, the inventory stratification plan, and the method of selecting the actual items to be verified;

- The extent to which cyclic, dynamic, or perpetual inventory data and production records, if any, will be used to modify or supplement the sample size, sample selection, or item verification procedures; and

- The minimum loss detection sensitivity and maximum time periods between item verifications for each item stratum of material.

In the Annex, provide the rationale for the item stratification plan.

Affirmations:

All items, not included in process monitoring will be included in the sample population stratification for item verification, unless exempted by §74.55(c). The appropriate power of detection and verification frequency will be used, based on category and specific item characteristics.

The presence and integrity of selected SSNM items are verified periodically. The item selection method has at least a 99% probability of detecting the loss of items plant-wide that total 5 FKG within:

- 30 calendar days from loss for Category IA items and 60 calendar days from a loss for Category IB items for items in a vault or a CAA that is isolated from the rest of the MAA,

- 3 working days from a loss for Category IA items and 7 calendar days from a loss for Category IB items located elsewhere in the MAA except for encapsulated components each measuring at least 1 meter in length and weighing in excess of 30 kilograms for which the time interval shall be 30 calendar days,

- 60 calendar days from the loss of Category IB items of waste stored in a permanently CAA outside of an MAA, and

- 60 calendar days for samples in a vault or CAA and 30 calendar days for samples elsewhere in the MAA for samples each containing less than 0.05 FKG of SSNM.

Acceptance Criteria:

When incorrect descriptive information for an item, such as item type, seal number, or location, is discovered, the action to be taken will ensure that the item is located, is correctly identified, and the deficiencies in the system are corrected.

In addition to positive identification and location confirmation, item verification includes: encapsulation integrity or container integrity checks, as appropriate; and tamper-safe seal integrity check, if appropriate. Considerations related to verification include the following:

- Electronic or optical methods such as bar code readers may be used in place of manual methods to record item or seal numbers provided safeguards against falsification are in place.

- If the licensee can demonstrate that seal falsification is noncredible, seal identification can be done on a random basis provided an independent means of confirming item identity, such as unique container numbers, is utilized.

- Seal integrity checks normally encompasses visual examination and, for certain seals (e.g., Type E), physical handling. Proposed shortcuts may be justified on the basis of low strategic value, limited accessibility, frequency of checks, and backup checks by production, quality assurance, production control, etc. These must be reviewed for acceptability on a case-by-case basis.

- The magnitude of the formal item verification effort can be adjusted to take credit for other means of confirming the presence and identity of sealed items. Process control and accounting, quality control testing, and other production operations routinely generate information that can serve to verify the identity and presence of sealed items. These sources can be used in lieu of item verification provided the frequency and loss detection sensitivity requirements of the item verification procedure are met and the use of the data for this purpose is not predictable. Examples of specific sources of such data are:

  1) Records that an item was created (tamper-safing procedure applied) or transferred within the required time span, as defined in §74.55(b),

  2) Records that an item was inspected, tested, analyzed, altered, or subjected to any other production or quality assurance operation within the required time span, and

  3) Production schedules showing that a particular item was "cued up" for production planning purposes where the cuing process involved a check of identity and location.

- Any tamper-safe or encapsulated items that have been verified by such a procedure within the time span required for that category of material can be exempted from formal item verification provided (i.e., only if): the prior handling or inspection activities, as indicated above, for which credit is being taken are unknown and unpredictable to a potential diverter, or if known or predictable, the items are scheduled to be physically accounted for by at least two individuals during sequential processing or inspection steps to occur during the next required test time span. To exempt such items from formal item verification, the items are simply dropped from the list of n items selected from the inventory list where n is the sample size required for verification.

The frequency of item verification tests is consistent with the maximum elapsed time intervals between the occurrence of a loss and its detection as specified in §74.55(b).

A physical inventory can serve in lieu of an item monitoring test provided all items represented by an item test are subject to verification as part of the physical inventory process, and further provided that:

a) by using the physical inventory in lieu of item monitoring tests, there is no extension in the maximum time interval between item monitoring tests for 3-day and 7-day tests; and

b) for 30-day and 60-day item tests, the physical inventory is completed within 33 calendar days and 66 calendar days, respectively, of the previous item test.

2.1.8 Sample Items

Describe the technique used to establish the sample population and how the presence of selected items will be verified. Additionally, describe how samples containing greater than 0.05 FKG will be monitored.

Affirmations:

Samples each containing less than 0.050 FKG will be included in the item monitoring program, provided they contain at least 0.001 FKG.

Acceptance Criteria:

Samples containing in excess of 0.05 FKG can be considered a sidestream in a bulk test performed in the originating process unit provided the samples are returned to process within 7 days. SSNM removals from such samples should be documented and the area records corrected accordingly.

Small items such as element sections and samples can be amassed in a tamper-safed container to alleviate excessive item verification. Conversely, items greater than 0.05 FKG should not be consolidated within a larger tamper-safe container for the primary purpose of reducing item verification effort.

The means of determining the number of items to be verified per class or stratum is specified. For example, the equation

$$n = N (1 - \beta^{1/d}) \quad \text{or} \quad n = N (1 - \beta^{x/G})$$

is an acceptable formula for calculating the sample size required from an inventory or any subset or group of size N, where d is the minimum number of altered or missing items (defects) that could total a goal quantity (i.e., 5 FKG) and $1 - \beta$ is the desired probability of obtaining at least one defect in the sample of n items where there are d defects ($d \geq 1$) in the population of N items. The number d is a function of the amount of SSNM per item. If the SSNM content varies over the population of items, the largest value must be used to calculate d to ensure that n is large enough to guarantee that the power of detection is at least 99%. This results in a conservative value of n, i.e., n is larger than necessary. If a smaller item content were chosen, such as the average value, an informed adversary could selectively divert only large items and thereby reduce the risk of detection. The 1/d exponent is equivalent to x/G (as shown in the alternative equation) where x is the maximum formula grams within a single item (for the stratum being tested) and G is the goal quantity.

Additional points to consider in this regard include the following:

- In those cases where the SSNM content per item is very small, the required sample size is a small fraction of the inventory. The result may even be that, in some instances the calculated sample size will be less than one. However, such items cannot be ignored. An acceptable approach would be to periodically verify one randomly selected item from the class at times chosen by random selection, such as by a random number generator.

- In some instances an entire stratum may contain less than 5 FKG. Nevertheless, such strata should be sampled like any other.

- If the number of items, N, in each strata remains reasonably constant (such as within 95 % to 105 % of a historical avcerage N) it is not necessary to recalculate the fraction of the population, n/N, to be checked each time.

- Neither the specific items to be verified in any particular instance nor items that won't be verified shall be predictable.

- Every item in a stratum has an equal probability of being selected for verification.

Items of IA type material may be treated as Category IB items and subject to the lower frequency item loss test if:

- The item is rigid and its dimensions are large enough to preclude hiding the item on an individual (i.e., at least 130 centimeters in 1 dimension, greater than 65 centimeters in each of 2 dimensions, or greater than 20 centermeters in each of 3 dimensions.),

- The weight of an item is so large that one person cannot carry the item inconspicuously. The minimum weight to meet this criterion is 50 kilograms, or

- The quantity of SSNM in the item is so small that a large number of diversions are needed to accumulate 5 FKG. The maximum quantity to meet this criterion is 50 formula grams per item.

The first two exceptions (for item test frequency), given above, do not apply if the item can be opened or disassembled and part or all of the SSNM removed without a high probability of being observed or detected.

The presence of very large (higher tier) components such as fuel blocks, preassemblies, subassemblies, etc., stored outside of a CAA must be verified in accordance with a sampling plan that provides the capability to detect a 5 FKG loss within 30 calendar days. One month is deemed to be acceptable on the basis of the large physical size and weight of these items and the restrictions on removing them from the MAA.

The number of items to be verified is sufficient to give a power of detection of at least 99% for a loss of items totaling 5 or more FKG from each stratum or inventory subdivision (a grouping into similar types and amounts of SSNM). If all strata in a facility are sampled for verification with at least a 99% power of detecting a loss of items containing 5 FKG, that criterion also will be achieved for a loss of items containing 5 FKG or more plant-wide.

The item inventory is stratified or subdivided in a manner that ensures at least a 99% power of detection while minimizing the number of items to be verified. It is advantageous to subdivide the inventory into classes or strata having approximately uniform quantities of SSNM per item. A moderate range of SSNM contents within a class, such as ± 10% to 20% is tolerable. However, regardless of the variability of SSNM content per item, the maximum item content (for the stratum in question) must be used when determining the minimum number of items that could constitute a 5 FKG loss (and hence determine the number of items that make up the sample size n). Typical classes for sampling are fuel elements, containers of scrap, containers of feed material, containers of waste, etc.

Encapsulated items containing less than 100 grams of SSNM whose presence has been verified during the prior 2 months as part of a statistical sample or handling during routine production need not be reverified for physical inventory. Items whose presence has not been verified in the same time interval should be located by two-person inventory teams.

Whenever an item monitoring test results in an MC&A alarm, a 5FKG (or greater) loss should be assumed until shown otherwise — either by additional (i.e., extra) item monitoring tests or by a physical inventory. See section 3.1, "Intent and Scope", for the definition of an item monitoring alarm. When verifying n randomly selected items for an item test, if one or more defective and/or missing items are encountered, an additional group of randomly selected items from the same stratum should be tested. In this additional test, the sample size should be twice as large (i.e., equal to 2n), and should not include any defective items from the initial test. Other strata scheduled for testing on the same date as the stratum giving rise to the alarm should also be subjected to additional testing (by using a 2n sample size instead of the normal size of n items). If the quantity of missing SSNM associated with the initial alarm is substantially less than 5 FKG and no further alarms result from the additional tests, strong evidence will have been obtained that a 5 FKG loss did not occur. If, on the other hand, one or more additional alarms are encountered, a complete physical inventory of all SSNM items should be immediately initiated. [Also see last paragraph of Section 3.1.4, pages 46 and 47.]

3.0 ALARM RESOLUTION

3.1 Alarm Resolution [§ 74.57(b), (d), (e), and (f)(1)]

Requirement

The rule requires that a licensee resolve the nature and cause of any MC&A alarm within an approved time period, or if not resolved within the approved time period, the licensee must notify the NRC that the alarm in question remained unresolved beyond the time period specified for its resolution. Such notification must occur within 24 hours following the expiration of the resolution period, except when a holiday or weekend intervenes, in which case the notification must occur on the next NRC scheduled workday. If a loss has occurred, the licensee is to determine the amount of SSNM lost and, as appropriate, return out-of-place SSNM to an appropriate place, update and correct involved records, and modify the MC&A system to prevent similar occurrences in the future. Additionally, if a process monitoring abrupt loss detection estimate exceeds 5 FKG of SSNM, material processing operations related to the alarm are to be suspended until completion of planned resolution activities unless the suspension of operations will negatively affect the ability to resolve the alarm. However, operations of continuous processes may continue for a 24-hour period while checks are made for mistakes.

Intent and Scope

The intent of these requirements is that the licensee's alarm resolution system must be able to respond promptly to alarms indicating a potential loss of SSNM and determine whether the alarm was caused by an actual loss or by a system error. The alarm resolution program also should be able to identify the type of system error or innocent cause so that remedial action can be taken. The alarm response should be timely to ensure that alarms are investigated and resolved promptly while memories of events leading up to the alarm are still fresh, materials are still available for remeasurement, and fewer changes of process conditions, inventories, in-process holdup, and item locations will have occurred. Prompt resolution will facilitate recovery of "lost" or stolen material.

For process monitoring, an MC&A alarm is defined as any material control test result that exceeds a defined alarm threshold value (such as that given on page 8 (Section 1.1.2) of this NUREG document. For item monitoring, an MC&A alarm exist whenever an item monitoring test results in (1) one or more item discrepancies (i.e., items not in their designated locations) which are not resolved within 8 hours for IA items, and 24 hours for IB items; or (2) one or more items being found defective (i.e., with some or all of their SSNM contents missing).

3.1.1 Alarm Resolution Procedures

Describe the alarm resolution procedures that will be applied to the various types of alarms and unit processes. The procedures should take into account credible innocent occurrences that may cause alarms indicating a potential SSNM loss. The resolution procedure descriptions may be abbreviated.

Also describe in the Plan the specific procedures to be employed in response to alarms indicating a potential loss in excess of 5 FKG. The description should identify those operations that will be shut down or alternative measures that will be employed in lieu of shutdown to facilitate an investigation.

In the Annex, provide:

- A listing of identified credible causes of possible alarms by unit process and details of the resolution procedures by which specific causes could be identified,

- A statistical estimate of the expected number of unresolvable alarms per inventory period with loss estimates greater than 5 FKG and a description of the estimation method, and

- The justification for not shutting down certain process operations during an investigation.

Affirmations:

Written investigation procedures are maintained that include decision rules by which a particular cause or combination of causes will be accepted as the cause of an alarm.

Acceptance Criteria:

Resolution procedures are described for alarms that indicate a potential abrupt loss of 5 FKG of SSNM in bulk or item form. The procedures take into account the expected differences in loss mechanisms and necessary differences in response approaches for in-process materials, items, different material types, and different types of unit operations. The differences and variations in resolution procedures are explained. Examples of different types of unit processes are:

- A bulk storage unit,

- A batch process with cleanout between batches and very small amounts of in-process holdup,

- A continuous process with continuous flow between the unit process and the succeeding process, and

- A process with large hold-up inventories that cannot be measured directly without cleanout.

The alarm resolution procedures provide a systematic and logical sequence of steps for determining the cause or causes of an alarm. An example of a systematic approach to assessment would be:

- Check the data and calculations for clerical, transcription, or computational errors,

- Trace the data to the primary sources (operator logbooks or production records and analytical reports) to check for agreement,

- Compare the source data, such as item and batch sizes and numbers, inventory quantities and flow rates, to historical values to detect anomalies that may indicate an error of identification or measurement,

- Review downstream material balances for potential off-setting gains,

- Localize the source of the alarm as nearly as possible with regard to time, place, material type, and individuals potentially involved,

- Report a potential SSNM loss to security who then should implement intensified search and surveillance procedures,

- Stop further processing in the unit process, if feasible, to retain items and inventory for remeasurement, and

- Remeasure all items, inventories, batches, and/or samples from the unit process that are still available.

Questions and Answers:

Q How do alarm resolution requirements [§74.57] integrate the contingency plans for MC&A events required in 10 CFR Part 73?

A Licensees' plans for response to MC&A indications of possible theft or missing SSNM are currently part of the licensees' "Safeguards Contingency Plans," required by 10 CFR 70.22(g)(2), 73.20(c), and 73.46(h). These were prepared in accordance with the criteria in Appendix C to 10 CFR Part 73 and Regulatory Guide 5.55, "Standard Format and Content of Safeguards Contingency Plans for Fuel Cycle Facilities." However, the regulations under which those plans were prepared and reviewed focused on the physical security system. The reform amendments define the performance to be achieved by the licensees in response to detection alarms from the MC&A system and to external allegations of thefts. Furthermore, the reform amendments require reconsideration by the licensee of what constitutes an MC&A detection, with increased attention paid to process and production anomalies that might be due to SSNM loss, and less emphasis on periodic physical inventories. Thus the licensees would have to periodically revise their FNMC plans to comply with the reform amendments, as well as reconsider the parts of their Safeguards Contingency Plans dealing with MC&A events. Rather than duplicate the same words in both plans, either plan could incorporate by reference appropriate pages of the other.

3.1.2 Decision Rules

Describe the types of information and data developed during response that will be accepted as sufficient evidence for assigning a specific cause to an alarm. The information and data described above should form the basis for development of the decision rules to be included in this section. These rules should take into account every identified potential innocent cause that may result in a bulk or item loss alarm.

Affirmations:

A systematic investigation into the nature and cause of each MC&A alarm will continue until the cause has been established or a determination has been made that the alarm is not resolvable with the information currently available. NRC will be notified when the latter situation occurs within 24 hours or within the next working day when a weekend or holiday intervenes.

Investigation of alarms is initiated promptly, and the maximum allowable time periods for completion of the alarm resolution procedures are specified in Section 3.1.1 (*Alarm Resolution Procedures*).

A search for a missing item continues until the item is either located or evidence is obtained that the item has been destroyed. A claim that an item containing more than 50 formula grams was destroyed without having been recorded is supported by independent and concrete confirmatory evidence of destruction.

Following alarm resolution, appropriate corrective action is taken to correct any records in error, to return misplaced SSNM to the proper location, if appropriate, and to revise the MC&A system to prevent similar occurrences in the future if such action is warranted.

When an actual loss of SSNM is indicated, the quantity of material lost is estimated and other information that may aid in the recovery of the material, such as the material type and container type and who last had responsibility for it, is generated, if possible.

When a detection alarm indicates a potential loss in excess of 5 FKG, continuous processing operations related to the alarm is suspended within 24 hours after the alarm, and the suspension is continued until completion of the planned resolution activities unless the suspension would negatively affect the ability to resolve the alarm,

or

When a detection alarm indicates a potential loss in excess of 5 FKG, batch processing operations are suspended immediately after the alarm or upon completion of the batch in process, and the suspension is continued until completion of the planned resolution activities.

When a process is not shut down, equally effective alternative measures are taken when an alarm occurs, to protect information and material that would be needed during the alarm investigation. Alternative measures by unit process are documented in the procedures specified in Section 3.1.1 (*Alarm Resolution Procedures*).

Acceptance Criteria:

Each type of alarm response is identified with the corresponding types of material and/or unit processes and the credible innocent causes of the alarm. Examples of innocent causes would be:

- A clerical or computational error is identified that clearly explains the alarm,

- A missing item is located,

- A claim that an item was added to the process, although no record of the transfer exists, if substantiated through an actual yield versus predicted yield comparison,

- A remeasurement confirms that error(s) in the original data caused the alarm, or

- A random fluctuation in the measurement process or a process variability is identified through sufficient measurements or additional processing.

The decision rules for a conclusion that a particular cause is applicable and that the alarm is resolved are described. (Backup information about the rationale and justifications are included in the Annex.) A decision rule must generally provide an objective basis for deciding whether or not the data and information acquired up to that point in the alarm assessment supports the hypothesis that the alarm was due to an innocent cause. Each decision rule should be based on the identification of a specific cause or a source of incorrect data that contributed to the alarm level of the loss estimator except that the rule may verify with high probability that no loss has occurred without having identified all contributing causes of the alarm. Examples of acceptable decision rules are:

- A false alarm resulting from a mistake.

    1) A correctable mistake identified and supported by direct evidence such as comparison to data collection sheets, reading a column level, or measuring a sample.

    2) A correctable mistake or recordkeeping error identified and supported by at least two sources of independent indirect evidence such as consistency of process values, historical ranges, a loss followed by a gain in the following control unit such that an error in the transfer was identified as greater than measurement error, or an interview with operators who observed an unusual process condition.

    3) A hypothesized uncorrectable mistake (or combination of mistakes) or procedural error which is supported by a difference of opposite sign and comparable magnitude in a related loss indicator and two sources of indirect evidence such as process yield, balance around non-SSNM materials, process consistency, or measurement control data indicating a short-term failure.

- A false alarm caused by stochastic fluctuations in the detection system.

    1) An error resulting from measurement variability identified and supported by remeasuring inventories or transfers where the differences between the original and remeasurement values exceed the 2-sigma confidence interval used to monitor and control measurement performance.

    2) An error resulting from variabilities in the process that is confirmed by processing the material through the process and verifying the discrepancy by recovering the material.

    3) An error resulting from inadequate modeling of in-process inventory where continued processing results in a stable cumulative loss indicator.

    4) A bias identified by an independent technique that results from differences in material types being processed.

Remeasurements of the SSNM to verify the content or composition of items or bulk material associated with an alarm are made to a standard deviation of the quantity estimate that is comparable to that of the book value, and the hypothesis that the difference between the initial and remeasurement value is zero is tested at the 0.05 level of significance.

After an alarm has been resolved, the planned corrective action includes MC&A system revisions, if appropriate, that provide reasonable assurance that future alarms of that nature (i.e., having the same or a similar cause) will not occur. An example of where an MC&A system revision would be appropriate would be revision of a procedure or computer software that contains an error that caused an alarm.

The operations that will be shut down to resolve alarms indicating a possible loss in excess of 5 FKG are identified or alternatives to shutdown are provided. [Refer to pages 8 and 9 for establishing alarm threshold values indicative of a possible 5 FKG loss.] Examples of acceptable alternatives might include:

- Shutting down of only downstream operations to retain products that may require remeasurement,

- Discontinuing the processing of certain sidestreams to retain scrap or recyclable intermediates that may require remeasurement,

- Diverting scrap, waste, or product from the alarming unit to auxiliary vessels or to a buffer storage area to retain the products for remeasurement,

- Collecting additional samples for remeasurement of materials that would become unavailable if operations were not suspended in the area under investigation.

- The key consideration in employing alternatives to shutdown is that the licensee can show that no data or information needed for response will be lost if the alternative is used.

The conditions for restart are specified. Fundamental to any decision to restart is whether the alarm has been resolved (i.e., an assignable cause has been identified), the loss is real but remedial, recovery action is underway, or the alarm has not been resolved. Prior to restart, the licensee must verify that all possible data associated with the process material have been acquired, and no information will be jeopardized by resuming operations.

The quality of the licensee's loss resolution capability is such that the combination of the material control test and resolution decisions permit alarms remaining unresolved after investigation to be good indicators of material loss. To achieve this objective, the licensee's planning data should demonstrate that the expected number of unresolved alarms in excess of 5 FKG are less than 0.10 abrupt loss alarms per inventory period.

The following additional information is pertinent to this point:

The only false alarms that need to be predicted are those due to normal process or measurement system statistical variation. Mistakes in transcription of data or process upsets do not need to be predicted because the response procedures should be designed to correctly resolve alarms stemming from those types of events. False alarms due to statistical fluctuations are expected to be more difficult to resolve.

One approach is to claim no credit for resolution of statistical alarms. Then the incremental expected number of alarms with discrepancies greater than 5 FKG can be calculated for a single test from the formula:

$$\Delta N = 1 - F\ (5/\sigma)$$

where

$\sigma = \quad$ the predicted standard deviation of the detection test in FKG

$F(x) = \quad$ the predicted statistical distribution of the test statistic normalized by σ.

This increment must then be multiplied by the expected number of times the test will be performed in an inventory period, and similar calculations then added up over all tests in the facility. That sum must be less than 0.10 (i.e., the number of such alarms would be less than one in 60 months, assuming a physical inventory frequency of every six months).

If the distribution function cannot be assumed to the normal (Gaussian) and the true distribution cannot be adequately predicted, the Camp-Meidell inequality may be applied if it is reasonable to expect the true distribution will be symmetric and unimodal (see Shewhart 1931, pages 176-177; and Eisenhart, Hastay and Wallis 1947, page 49). The Camp-Meidell inequality permits a bound on N to be calculated from the formula:

$$\Delta N \quad \leq \quad (\frac{8}{9})(\frac{\sigma}{10})^2$$

where σ has units of formula kilograms. However, this will typically be useful only if σ is less than 0.1 FKG. A more useful approach would be to estimate the maximum range that the test statistic could be based on a physical model of the process and measurement systems under the hypothesis of no material diversion. If this value is less than 5 FKG, set $\Delta N = 0$.

Evaluation is more complicated if the licensee claims that response procedures will permit resolution of some fraction of the statistical false alarms. Such procedures would need to be summarized in the plan. One approach is to make additional measurements of inputs, products, sidestreams, and holdups to complete measured material balances where loss detectors are based on average expected yields. Additional measurement of input quantities requires samples to be taken and retained. This would permit laboratory analyses to be made which are more reliable than NDA. The procedures also could utilize data resulting from processing the same batch through the next process step, data resulting from processing another batch through the same process step, and tests that eliminate intermediate measurement points by combining several process steps. In any of these, estimating the fraction of N that would be expected to remain unresolved requires detailed modeling of the response capability.

A Monte Carlo simulation method can be used to model the alarm response procedures and predict the resolution success rate. For a single material control test, refer to Tanner (1981). For an entire plant, refer to Reardon, Heaberlin and Eggers (1982). Detailed information is available in Eggers (1982).

Alternatively, if the licensee has a performance history of responses to and assessment of alarms, this may be cited in-place of the simulation of a proposed response program if the experience demonstrates a capability to meet the commitment goals for resolving false alarms.

Questions and Answers:

Q What quality of loss resolution must the licensee achieve?

A The combined quality of the material control test and loss resolution decisions shall permit alarms remaining unresolved after completion of the licensee's investigative activities to be good indicators of theft or diversion. This will be judged in two ways:

1) During review of a licensee's planned detection and alarm resolution capabilities, attention will be directed to the ability to resolve false abrupt loss alarms. For the alarm resolution capability to be acceptable, it must appear able

to correctly identify all errors due to leaks, process upsets, or human mistakes that are large enough to cause an alarm. With respect to other false alarms, in particular those alarms that are expected to occur because of the statistical nature of the processes and measurement systems, the alarm resolution capability need not be 100% effective. However, for it to be acceptable, it must be effective enough to satisfactorily limit the statistically expected rate of unresolvable abrupt loss alarms. (The expected rate can be thought of as a weighted average of all possible rates, where the weights are the likelihoods of occurrence of those rates.) A satisfactory limit is an expected rate of unresolvable large abrupt loss alarms less than one per 10 years per plant. A large false alarm is one whose loss estimate exceeds 5 FKG. Because the licensee should be able to resolve all such alarms other than those of a statistical nature, calculation of the expected rate of unresolvable large abrupt loss false alarms needs only consider false alarms of a statistical nature.

2) After the phase-in period is over and all elements of the licensee's alarm resolution commitments have been implemented, the alarm resolution performance would be judged good when: (a) there have been no situations over the past year in which subsequent audits or investigations determined that a large abrupt loss alarm was innocently caused but not resolved within the licensee's time commitments; and (b) there are no unresolved large abrupt loss alarms remaining after the bi-monthly inventories and annual audit have been completed.

3.1.3 Response Time

Indicate the response times that will be allotted to resolve each alarm type. If alarms involving certain material types or alarms from certain processes require appreciably longer response times than those estimated in the acceptance criteria section below, justify the indicated times.

Affirmations:

Loss detection alarms will be resolved as promptly as practical given the process complexity.

Acceptance Criteria:

The alarm resolution time commitments ensure a reasonably prompt alarm response. The check of the loss indicator data for clerical mistakes and data errors should normally be completed within 24 hours for any abrupt loss alarm. The maximum time for completion of the resolution procedure for alarms indicating a possible abrupt loss of items that were tamper-safed, encapsulated, or retained in a vault that provided protection equivalent to tamper-safing should normally not exceed 3 calendar days. The maximum time for completion of the resolution procedure for alarms indicating a possible abrupt, loss of SSNM in any form or container that was not tamper-safed, encapsulated, or stored in a vault equivalent to tamper-safing should not normally exceed 3 working days. However, if longer time periods are required for certain unit processes or types of necessary response activities, the licensee should explain and justify the proposed times in its submitted FNMC plan.

When a tamper-safed or encapsulated item has been compromised, a remeasurement must be undertaken immediately. The maximum time after the alarm for completing a remeasurement to confirm the contents should normally not exceed 2 working days. Any proposed extension of that time should be explained and justified. An example of where additional time might be necessary would be if isotopic measurements are performed off-site.

When a vault or CAA providing protection equivalent to tamper-safing has been entered without authorization, when the prescribed vault protection has been compromised, or when other indications of loss of control are discovered, the entire vault contents must be accounted for within 3 calendar days by a piece count and attribute test of all items not tamper-safed or encapsulated, such as by weighing or NDA. Remeasurement of all items in the vault or CAA not tamper-safed or encapsulated should be initiated within 1 working day. If a longer period is proposed, justification is provided.

3.1.4 Item Discrepancies

Describe the actions that will be taken in response to the following item discrepancies:

* An item has apparently been destroyed without being recorded.

* The integrity of a tamper-safed or encapsulated item has been compromised.

* Unauthorized entry or other violation of control of a vault or a permanently CAA has occurred.

* A statistically significant difference between the measured input and output value of an untamper-safed item placed in vault or CAA storage has been detected, and such difference exceeds 25 grams SSNM.

The actions in response to these discrepancies should include decision rules which will be the basis of acceptable resolution.

Affirmations: If the integrity of an item has been compromised (i.e., the container seal or the encapsulation has been altered or broken) an appropriate response procedure is promptly initiated to determine whether any SSNM is missing.

Compromised items are placed under surveillance or in secure storage and are remeasured within specified time periods. The quality of the remeasurement is at least equal to that of the original measurement.

Acceptance Criteria: An item loss assessment procedure has been included that details a logical sequence of actions to resolve an apparent loss. A typical assessment sequence (not necessarily in the order listed) might be to:

- Determine that the records are apparently correct by tracing the item identification and location information to its source data in inventory and production records;

- Search other production and storage areas to determine if the item was transferred without supporting documentation;

- Identify all persons involved in creation and movement of the item(s) and question them for possible ways the item might have been misplaced or record errors made;

- Extend the search to other locations, particularly those suggested by the persons involved;

- Check for possible errors in the item records by evaluating the bulk material balances in the adjacent processing units;

- Reinventory all items of that type in storage locations routinely used for such items; and

- Extend the inventory search to items of similar size and appearance.

A description of the licensee's proposed course of action in response to broken tamper-seal should include:

- Placing the item under surveillance immediately or in secured storage and remeasuring it as soon as practicable (time limits specified) to determine if SSNM is missing,

- Performing blending, mixing, or splitting operations, if appropriate, to ensure that any samples taken for remeasurement are representative; and

- Comparing (testing) the difference between the original and confirmation measurement for statistical significance with a probability of no more than 5% of concluding that no SSNM is missing when in fact a loss has occurred. The quality of the remeasurement should be at least equivalent to the original measurement.

If the cause of the alarm is claimed to be the destruction of an item such as by processing it to another form, without the act having been recorded, confirmatory evidence must be developed to support the conclusion. The types of confirmatory evidence that are expected to be applicable are described in the plan. The evidence will be acceptable if it is relevant, concrete, independent, and objective. Examples of such evidence are:

- The measured density of a suspect solution is consistent with the predicted density assuming the contents of the missing container had been added to the process,

- The actual yield from a suspect unit process is consistent with the predicted yield from that process if it contained the contents of the missing item, or

- The fact that the container was added to process can be attested to by two individuals.

If an item is discovered as not being in its recorded location, such an event should be designated as an *item discrepancy* (with the time of such discovery being documented). If an item discrepancy is not resolved within 8 hours for IA items, and within 24 hours for IB items, an alarm is declared. The licensee normally declares such an item as *missing* if not found or accounted for within: 24 hours for Category IA items and 3 working days for all other items (relative to time that item discrepancy was discovered). A search for a misplaced item that was not tamper-safed or encapsulated may not be terminated without NRC permission until the item is located or evidence of its destruction is obtained. A claim that an item was destroyed without recording the fact may be accepted if independent confirmatory evidence of destruction is obtained. Items containing less than 0.05 FKG are exempted from the requirements for confirmatory evidence. Searches for declared missing items may not be interrupted by idle time such as weekends and holidays.

If an item is discovered as being compromised and more than 25 grams of SSNM is missing from the item, an MC&A alarm should be immediately declared.
Whenever an item monitoring test results in an MC&A alarm, a 5

FKG (or greater) loss should be assumed until shown otherwise, either by additional (i.e., extra) item monitoring tests or by a physical inventory. If, when verifying n randomly selected items for an item test, one or more defects are encountered and the quantity of missing SSNM associated with the compromised or missing items is substantially less than 5 FKG, an immediate additional group of randomly selected items from the same statum should be tested. In this additional test, the sample size should be twice as large (i.e., equal to 2n), and should not include any of the defective items from the initial test. If no alarm results upon performing the additional 2n test, strong evidence will have been obtained that a 5 FKG loss from the stratum in question did not occur. Depending on the circumstances, additional item tests on other strata may be necessary in order to resolve an item alarm. If the quantity of missing SSNM associated with the initial alarm is 4.000 or more (i.e., not substantially less than 5 FKG), a physical inventory of all items on hand should be immediately initiated. [Also see last paragraph of Section 2.1.8, page 33.]

3.2 Alarm Reporting [§74.57(c) and (f)(2)]

Requirement

The rule requires that a licensee notify the appropriate NRC safeguards licensing organization within the Office of Nuclear Materrial Safety and Safeguards of any MC&A alarm that remains unresolved beyond the time period specified for its resolution. Notification is to occur within 24 hours following the deadline for resolution, or by the next working day when a weekend or holiday intervene. For alarm estimates that exceed 5 FKG, the notification that an MC&A alarm resolution procedure has been initiated is to occur within 24 hours of the alarm occurance.

Intent and Scope

The intent of these requirements is that the NRC be made aware of potential SSNM losses in a timely manner so that appropriate actions can be initiated.

3.2.1 Reporting Responsibility

Indicate how the responsibility for reporting unresolved alarms will be assigned in the organization.

Affirmations:

The appropriate NRC Office will be notified within 24 hours, or by the next workday when a weekend or holiday intervene, of any alarm that remains unresolved beyond the time limit specified for its resolution in Section 3.1.3 (*Response Time*).

The appropriate NRC Office will be notified within 24 hours of the initiation of an alarm resolution procedure involving an alarm estimate that exceeds 5 FKG.

Acceptance Criteria: The responsibility for reporting unresolved alarms is assigned at a sufficiently high level of responsibility within the licensee's organization that decisions on the need for reporting will be timely and unquestioned.

With regard to recurring losses, a significant loss trend is reported to the NRC within 1 week of its discovery and the progress of the resulting investigation is reported monthly.

3.2.2 *Information*

Discuss the types of information that will be provided to NRC and the schedule for updating the status of the unresolved alarms to NRC.

Affirmations: The NRC Office will be provided with current, technically defensible information on the status of alarm resolution activities based on a mutually agreed upon schedule.

Acceptance Criteria: The information to be reported includes: the magnitude of the discrepancy indicated by the alarm, the investigation procedure, the status of the investigation, the status of the facility, the planned remedial measures, and the status of the physical security system during the period.

The remedial measures include assignment of responsibility for the investigation to a technically competent individual, rechecking the response of the measurement system with certified standards, outlining a schedule of recalibrations of the key measurement systems if appropriate, in-situ or cleanout measurements of holdup, and statistical evaluation of the material accounting data.

3.3 Alleged Thefts [§74.57(e)]

Requirement The rule requires that a licensee establish and maintain ability to respond rapidly to alleged thefts.

Intent and Scope The intent of this requirement is to have an established capability to respond rapidly to alarms occurring external to the MC&A system. The response capability should provide the information necessary to rapidly assess the validity of an alleged theft.

3.3.1 *Response Capabilities*

Describe the item control system that will be maintained in order to readily determine the identity, quantity, and location of SSNM in item form. The description should include the forms, records, and document flow paths. Where records are not centralized, the means of record verification by MC&A personnel and the responsibility for maintenance and disposition should be described.

Describe the emergency physical inventory procedure, including a description of the status that each unit operation should be in to be inventoried and indicate the status of each unit operation during its inventory.

In the Annex provide estimates of the times needed to perform and reconcile the inventory and to determine the associated projected variance.

Affirmations: An allegation or other indication of diversion of SSNM from its authorized location will be rapidly investigated and evidence developed that supports either a confirmation or a denial.

A contingency capability is maintained to locate on demand any specific tamper-safed or encapsulated item or an unencapsulated item stored in a vault equivalent to tamper-safing within 8 hours, and to verify the presence of all items in a vault within 72 hours.

A contingency capability is maintained to initiate an emergency physical inventory of all SSNM in the plant, or in any portion of the plant, within 24 hours after receipt of an NRC order. ("Initiate" means to begin actions to place SSNM in a measurable form and perform necessary preparations for conducting a physical inventory.)

Acceptance Criteria: From the description of the SSNM item record system, it is evident that the records of the identity and location of every item can be updated with sufficient speed to support the commitments that any randomly selected item within a vault can be located within 8 hours, and any item outside a vault can be located within 24 hours. The capability also exists to locate all items within a vault within 72 hours and all items outside a vault or permanently CAA within 1 week.

Provisions are included for maintaining the availability of forms, tags, trained personnel, inventory listing, and other items that may be needed to initiate a plant-wide physical inventory within 24 hours. The emergency inventory capability is designed to help answer the following questions:

• Can it be determined conclusively that SSNM is or is not missing from the facility?

• What quantity is missing?

• What material type is it? For example, what is its isotopic composition, its chemical form, and its physical size?

• Over what time period could it have been diverted?

- Which plant employees or other individuals might have had access to it during that time?

- Which plant employees may be able to provide information useful for its recovery?

3.3.2 Record Maintenance

Describe the protective measures that will be implemented to prevent loss, misplacement, or accidental destruction of inventory and item location records. (Reference Section 4.6.2 *Record Maintenance.*)

Affirmations:

Accurate item inventory records are established and maintained to provide knowledge of the identity, location, and quantity of SSNM in the form of items outside a vault or CAA, and the capability is maintained to update the records rapidly enough to confirm the presence and integrity of any item within 24 hours and, upon demand, all items within 1 week.

For material not in the form of items, accurate records are established and maintained on the quantities of SSNM which have been received, shipped, or otherwise removed from each MAA, and quantities of SSNM remaining within each MAA. The capability will be maintained to update the records rapidly enough to meet the requirements for an emergency plant-wide physical inventory.

Acceptance Criteria:

Appropriate safeguards are implemented to prevent loss, misplacement, or accidental destruction of the inventory and item location records.

The data collecting, recording, and auditing procedures provide reasonable protection against errors in the records.

Questions and Answers:

Q   What are alleged thefts? [§74.57(e)]

A   Alarms that originate external to the MC&A system. Among these are any statements communicated directly or indirectly to facility staff, NRC, FBI, police, etc., that diversion of SSNM under license has occurred. The statements may or may not include details such as the plant area from which SSNM was allegedly taken, which item(s) was (were) taken, a description of the container(s) or material allegedly taken, or other information in support of the allegation. This covers threats allegedly from within as well as from outside the facility. An external alarm may include other indications such as an external assault that penetrated an MAA or the discovery that an MAA door had been opened from the inside.

4.0 QUALITY ASSURANCE

4.1 Management Structure [§74.59(b)]

Requirement

Establish and maintain a management structure that includes clearly defined responsibility for the planning, coordination, and administration of MC&A functions; independence of MC&A functions from production responsibilities; and separation of functions such that the activities of one individual or organizational unit serve as controls over and checks of the activities of others.

Provide for the adequate review and use of those MC&A procedures that are identified in the approved FNMC plan as being critical to the effectiveness of the described system.

Intent and Scope

The intent of this section is to require licensees to implement a management structure that permits effective functioning of the MC&A system. Documentation, review, and approval of the procedures and the assignment of the key functions to specific positions eliminates ambiguities about what is to be done by whom. The management structure is meant to separate key MC&A functions from each other in order to provide cross-checks that increase MC&A system reliability and counter defeat of the system through neglect, deceit, or falsification, and to free MC&A·management from conflicts of interest with other major responsibilities such as production.

4.1.1 Organization

Describe the organization for MC&A including the functional responsibilities for each organizational unit and show how the MC&A organization is independent of responsibilities that have potentially conflicting goals.

Affirmations:

The overall responsibility for the MC&A system is assigned to a management position that provides separation from production responsibilities or any other responsibilities that may give rise to a conflict of interest.

The responsibility for each MC&A function is assigned to a specific position in the organization in a way that key functions are cross-checked.

Acceptance Criteria:

The MC&A organization is separate from the SSNM production (operations) organization and any other organization that generates source data. Otherwise controls are in place to ensure that process operations, measurements, measurement controls, accounting functions, and any other activities that influence MC&A system performance are carried out both in the letter and spirit of approved procedures; and that decisions impacting MC&A, which can conflict with production or other plant functions, are under the oversight of an independent authority.

The management structure exhibits at least the following attributes:

- The overall planning, coordination, and administration of the MC&A functions for SSNM is vested in a single individual at an organizational level that is sufficient to ensure independence of action and objectivity of decisions. The individual must be in a position to recommend and initiate timely action for the control and accounting of SSNM including delaying production, if necessary, and must not be enmeshed in a hierarchical framework that could inhibit or compromise independent action.

- The assignment of MC&A functions in the licensee organization provides a separation of functions so that the activities of one individual or organizational unit serve as controls over and checks of the activities of other individuals or organizational units.

- The critical MC&A functions and activities are documented in written procedures. The procedures and any revision thereto are reviewed and approved by appropriate management personnel prior to implementation. The individual with overall responsibility for the MC&A system will approve all procedures generated in the MC&A organization and be cognizant of all other procedures affecting MC&A.

- Critical MC&A procedures should, as a minimum, address (1) the establishment of basic MC&A system policies; (2) measurement requirements and methodolgies; (3) detecting the loss of a goal quantity; (4) alarm resolution activities; (5) performance of the physical inventories; (6) determination of inventory and shipper-receiver differences; (7) establishment of measurement control policies; and (8) determination of measurement uncertainties and the standard error of inventory difference.

The responsibilities and authorities for each position assigned an SSNM control and accounting function are clearly defined in position descriptions that are accessible to all affected personnel and to the NRC upon request.

The individuals responsible for each MC&A function have sufficient authority to perform the function in the prescribed manner.

The overall management responsibility for the MC&A system is at a level at least comparable to the organization having responsibility for production or storage of SSNM, or a direct line of communication is provided to the management level which has the authority to implement measures essential to effective MC&A.

The individuals who generate source data, such as those performing measurements, preparing transfer forms, or preparing analytical reports do not perform any accounting or record control functions unless cross-checks of the work are performed to prevent falsification. Examples of appropriate checks and balances are:

- Review of measurement data and calculations by another individual,

- Maintenance of a duplicate copy of all source data and transfer forms under controls separate from the accounting function,

- Performance of independent audits, and

- Separation of computer program maintenance from the program user function.

No individual has the sole authority to recheck, evaluate, or audit information for which that individual is responsible.

No individual may have responsibility and control of both MC&A and physical protection functions unless independent cross-checks are in place to preclude defeat of the overall safeguards system. As a minimum, the cross-check must include countersigning by one other person of any SSNM transfer within an MAA and countersigning by two individuals for SSNM transfers out of an MAA.

The management structure provides for assignment of a responsibility for SSNM undergoing processing and in storage to a single individual or group. The duties of the individual(s) include but are not limited to:

- Maintaining appropriate inventory control over SSNM in their assigned area,

- Authorizing and recording all movements of SSNM into and out of their assigned area,

- Maintaining appropriate local MC&A records or ensuring that other records, such as production records, contain necessary MC&A information,

- Participating in physical inventories as required,

- Assisting in internal or external alarm resolution activities as required,

- Ensuring that, when SSNM is processed in bulk form, only authorized persons have hands-on access to the material, and

- Notifying proper authorities of irregularities in material and MC&A data handling.

4.1.2 Policies and Procedures

Describe the policies, procedures, duties, responsibilities, and authorities associated with each position involved with an MC&A function in sufficient detail to demonstrate the cross-checks built into the MC&A system.

In the plan provide a listing (by title and procedure number) of the procedures deemed to be critical to the effectiveness of the MC&A system.

Affirmations:

The management structure and the critical MC&A policies and procedures are documented and provisions are made for review and approval prior to implementation.

Acceptance Criteria:

Policies have been developed and documented to direct MC&A activities, including generation of procedures. Plant policies are periodically reviewed and revised as appropriate.

Procedures have been developed as specified in Section 4.9.1 (*MC&A Procedures*).

Questions and Answers:

Q   At what level of understanding should MC&A procedures be written?

A   Procedures such as those used in MC&A should be written so that any person performing the work should be able to understand the content and meaning of the actions to be taken, the warning statements, and all other messages. Generally, a twelfth grade level of vocabulary should be used in writing procedures. This restriction does not apply to the technical terminology included in the procedures, although these terms must then be included in any specific training that involved personnel are required to take.

Q What is a systematic task analysis, and how will it help to define the content of procedures?

A A task analysis breaks down and systematically evaluates a human function in terms of the abilities, skills, knowledge, and attitudes required for performance of the function. These analyses may be performed to differing degrees of depth, depending on the information requirement and its specific application.

A task analysis will assist the procedure developer by systematically outlining the steps to be performed to complete a task, the personnel needed to complete each step, and the requirements of each person.

Procedures usually do not require an in-depth task analysis, but consideration of the needs of personnel will usually make procedures better.

Q Why should procedures be reviewed and verified before being accepted for regular usage?

A Procedures that contain inaccurate or incomplete information are misleading and can be detrimental to MC&A information error rates. Personnel who have previously performed similar tasks or are familiar with the process to be performed will frequently discover omissions of required information, misleading information, or mistakes.

Verification of the procedures involves field testing by the personnel who will be using the procedures to determine problems not found during the review phase.

4.2 Personnel Qualification and Training [§74.59(c)]

Requirement   The rule requires that each licensee ensure that key personnel, who work in positions involving tasks where mistakes could directly degrade the safeguards capabilities of the MC&A system, are trained to maintain a high level of safeguards awareness and are qualified to perform their jobs.

Intent and Scope   The intent of this section is to ensure that the effectiveness of the MC&A system is maintained by the qualification and training of key personnel. A training and qualification program can help ensure that these individuals are adequately prepared to perform their functions correctly with a minimum of errors. The program should be structured to define job requirements, to

55

establish minimum qualifications for candidates, to train and qualify the candidates, and to define requalification criteria.

4.2.1 Training Program

Describe the fundamentals of the training program that will be implemented to ensure the competency of key MC&A personnel. The description should identify the training program structure, source of instructional material, and general training objectives.

In the Annex, provide an example of a typical training program for one typical position and a tabulation of the key MC&A positions.

Affirmations:

The duties, responsibilities, essential functions, and qualifications of key MC&A positions, i.e., those involving tasks where mistakes could directly degrade the safeguards capabilities of the MC&A system, are defined in written job descriptions.

A training and qualification program for key MC&A positions and a method of demonstrating continued competency of personnel have been implemented and will be maintained. The program is periodically updated to reflect changes in job requirements.

The descriptions of the key job functions, the design of the training and qualification program, and the method of confirming qualifications of personnel are subject to the formal approval of the MC&A manager.

Acceptance Criteria:

The list of key positions or functions includes all those for which errors or faulty performance could directly degrade SSNM control and accounting. These include MC&A management positions and individual contributor positions having responsibility for key measurements, data analysis, preparation of accountability source documents, and collecting or recording of other data having a direct impact on loss detection, alarm response, and quality assurance functions.

The training program emphasizes the job purpose and scope; relationship to other positions, especially the MC&A positions; the role or significance with respect to MC&A; technical knowledge; understanding of duties, responsibilities, and procedures; and skill development.

The training plans provide for a reasonable balance of theory and practice, or oral and written instruction versus demonstration and learning-by-doing, the use of on-job training for positions that are primarily operational or clerical, and

56

individualized instruction based on performance goals whenever feasible.

The training program provides for training of personnel already experienced and functioning in MC&A positions when competency tests indicate that additional training is called for. The criterion will be whether or not the individual can function at the level of proficiency called for in the qualification criteria.

4.2.2 Qualification Program

Describe the qualification program including generic qualification criteria for the key MC&A positions and the criteria for assessing the need for requalification.

In the Annex, provide an example of the complete qualification criteria for a key MC&A position.

Affirmations:

The continuing qualification of key personnel will be verified on an ongoing basis or at least every 2 years.
The individuals designated for key positions do not assume the positions until they have demonstrated their competence through tests that will determine whether or not the individual satisfies the preestablished qualification criteria for the positions.

Acceptance Criteria:

The qualification criteria for the key positions are consistent with the position descriptions and focus on minimum levels of education and experience, knowledge of the job content and its purposes, types and levels of skills or proficiencies, and understanding of the safeguards role and its importance. The criteria are defined in terms of measurable performance goals whenever possible.

Tests for positions requiring measurements, calculations, or recording of data and information will include demonstration of correct and accurate job performance. When operating procedures or manipulative skills are required, the tests will include hands-on demonstrations on competence.

4.3 Measurements [§74.59(d)]

Requirement

The rule requires that a licensee establish and maintain a system of measurements sufficient to:

1) Substantiate the element and fissile isotope content of all SSNM received, produced, and transferred between areas of custodial responsibility, on inventory, or shipped, discarded, or otherwise removed from inventory;

2) Provide the necessary data for the performance of the material control tests required by §74.53(b)(2);

3) Permit an estimation of the standard deviations associated with each measured quantity.

Intent and Scope

The intent of these requirements is that all SSNM values used for MC&A purposes be based on measurements and the uncertainties associated with the measured values be quantifiable.

4.3.1 Measurement Points

Identify each point in the process where measurements are made for SNM control and accounting purposes. References to process flow diagrams included in the Annex are acceptable.

Affirmations:

Measurement systems are maintained and utilized to substantiate the element and isotope content of all SSNM received, produced, transferred between areas of custodial responsibility, on inventory, or shipped, discarded, or otherwise removed from inventory.

SSNM quantities transferred into and out of each unit process are based on measurements for mass, volume, element, and isotope, as necessary, to accommodate material loss detection tests.

Acceptance Criteria:

All measurement points have been identified and as a minimum include the following:

• Facility receipts,

• Transfers between areas of custodial responsibility,

• Points where SSNM product or intermediate products are produced,

• Unit process boundaries,

• Facility shipments including product, scrap, and waste,

• Effluent discharge points, and

• Significant sidestreams.

4.3.2 Materials and Measurements

Characterize the materials and measurements for each measurement point. One suitable means of presentation would be a coded chart showing the types of materials and the components of measurement involved at each measurement point (i.e., weight, volume, sampling, analytical assay, or NDA).

In the Annex provide a detailed description of each measurement system employed for MC&A purposes. The description should include:

- General characteristics (equipment, range of application and sensitivity),

- Method description, and

- Estimated measurement uncertainties (random and systematic).

Affirmations: Measurement methods are appropriate for the matrix and SSNM characteristics of the material measured.

Factors employed in process models are based on measurements and are updated at least annually.

Acceptance Criteria: The material types to be measured at each measurement point and the measurement system involved are described in the Plan. Each "measurement system" should be defined or identified by its unique set of the following parameters:

- Measurement device or equipment,

- Standards used for calibration,

- Standards used for control,

- Sampling technique and apparatus (if applicable),

- Sample aliquoting technique (if applicable), and

- Sample aliquot pretreatment methodology (if applicable).

The descriptions of the components of each measurement system reflected in the Annex should include:

- Synopsis of technique,

- Range of application,

- Sensitivity,

- Precautions, and

- Random/fixed error estimates.

The use of factors is acceptable whenever the uncertainty associated with the factor is smaller than the random error of an applicable process material (or item) measurement. Otherwise, the use of factors should be limited to those situations where timely measurements are impractical. A commitment should be included to the effect that factors will be based on measurements, will be monitored, and updated when appropriate statistical tests indicate the need for updating. In the Annex, the licensee has justified the use of factors in lieu of measurements.

The acceptability of applying nominal (or historic) SSNM factors to measurements of mass, volume, or density for material control tests will depend upon the following considerations:

- Availability of substitute materials,

- Predictability of material composition, and

- Material accessibility

These considerations influence whether a test as simple as a weight comparison will suffice as a means of loss detection or if a measurement for element and perhaps isotope is necessary.

4.4 Measurement Control [§74.59(e)]

Requirements   The rule requires that a licensee ensure that the quality of SSNM measurement systems and material processing practices is continually controlled to a level of effectiveness sufficient to satisfy the capabilities required for detection, response, and accounting. To achieve this objective, the license should:

1) Perform engineering analyses and evaluations of the design installation, preoperational tests, calibration and operation of all measurement systems to be used for MC&A purposes.

2) Perform process and engineering tests using well characterized materials to establish or to verify the applicability of existing procedures for mixing and sampling SSNM and maintaining sample integrity during transport and storage.

3) Generate current data on the performance of measurement processes, including, as appropriate, values for bias corrections, uncertainties on calibration factors, and random error standard deviations. The program shall include:

- The ongoing use of standards for calibration and control of all applicable measurement systems. Calibrations shall be repeated whenever any significant change occurs in a measurement system or when program data, generated by tests performed at a predetermined frequency, indicate a need for recalibration. Calibrations and control standard measurements shall be based on standards with traceability to a national standard or nationally accepted measurement system.

- A system of control measurements to provide current data for the determination of random errors and bias estimates that are significant contributors to the measurement uncertainties associated with shipper-receiver differences, inventory differences, and process differences.

4) Utilize the measurement control data generated during the current material balance period for the estimation of the standard error of the inventory difference (SEID) and the standard deviations associated with the process differences. Measurement error data collected and used during immediately preceding material balance periods (up to six months prior to the current period) may be combined with current data provided that the measurement systems are in statistical control, and it can be shown by a statistical test that the combined data are all from the same population.

5) Evaluate all program data and information to ensure that measurement performance is so controlled that the SEID estimator is less than 0.1% of active inventory for SSNM processing facilities.

6) Apply bias corrections by an appropriate procedure whereby:

- Bias corrections are applied to individual items whenever the relative bias estimate exceeds twice the estimated standard deviation of the estimator and the absolute bias estimate also exceeds the rounding error (associated with an item's accounting ledger entry) of affected items.

- The impact of all biases, which are not applied as corrections to individual items, are applied as a correction to the inventory difference, if the net effect of all such biases exceeds 50 grams of SSNM.

61

7) Investigate and take corrective action, as appropriate, to identify and reduce associated measurement bias when, for a given material type, shipper/receiver differences accumulated over a 6 month period exceed the larger of 1 FKG or 0.1% of the total amount received.

8) Establish and maintain a statistical control system designed to monitor the quality of each type of program measurement. Control limits shall be established to be equivalent to levels of significance of 0.05 and 0.001. Control data exceeding the 0.05 limits shall be investigated and corrective action taken in a timely manner. Whenever data exceed the 0.001 control limit, the measurement system shall not be used for MC&A purposes until it has been brought into control at the 0.05 level.

Intent and Scope

The intent of these requirements is that the licensee continually control the quality of measurement systems employed for MC&A to a level sufficient to satisfy the capabilities required for loss detection, response, and accounting. The goals of the quality control program for SSNM measurements are to maintain the SEID within the limits specified in §74.59(e)(5) and minimize the measurement error contribution to the standard deviations associated with the material control tests required by §74.53(b).

4.4.1 Common Measurement Control Practices

Describe the general elements of the measurement control program applicable to those measurement systems used for MC&A. The description should include:

• The general types of standards that will be utilized,

• The procedure for certifying the values assigned to the standards,

• The minimum number and analysis frequency or schedule of control standard measurements and repplicate sample analyses of process materials that will be used to establish the magnitude of biases, calibration and control measurement errors, and variances of random errors,

• The means of monitoring the magnitude of biases and variances,

• The criteria for determining the need for recalibration,

• The means of establishing mixing and sampling errors,

- The tests and criteria for judging the acceptability of data pooling,

- The measures to ensure that bias estimates and variances reflect the actual operating conditions and process materials,

- The tests that will be employed to identify outliers, and

- The tests for assessing the significance of bias estimates.

In the Annex provide:

- A listing of the standards to be used with each measurement system and, for in-house standards, how they are prepared,

- A brief description of how assigned values of standards are determined,

- A brief description of the calibration procedures for each measurement system, and

- A listing of expected or estimated variances associated with each measurement system.

Affirmations: Analyses and evaluations are performed on the design, installation, preoperational testing, calibration, and operation of all measurement systems to be used for MC&A purposes.

Process and engineering tests are performed, using well characterized materials, to verify the applicability of mixing and sampling procedures for SSNM and ensure sample validity during transport and storage.

Current data are generated during the inventory period for establishing bias correction values, uncertainties on calibration factors, and random error variances.

Bias corrections are applied to individual items whenever a bias estimate exceeds twice the estimated standard deviation of the estimator and the rounding error of affected items. Otherwise the impact of biases is applied as a correction to the inventory difference. Bias correction adjustments to inventory difference are not entered in the accounting ledgers.

Bias corrections associated with material control tests are either applied prior to assessing the significance of the test results or are available for alarm resolution.

63

When a statistically significant change occurs in the estimated standard deviation of a material control test statistic, the alarm threshold of the test is adjusted as necessary to ensure that a goal quantity loss of SSNM will be detected with a probability at least as high as that required in the regulations [§74.53(b)(2)]. Additionally, the change will be investigated to an extent sufficient to determine the cause.

Contractors who perform MC&A measurement services will implement and maintain a control program for measurement uncertainties and for human errors. The program will be of such depth and intensity to preclude any degradation of the MC&A system.

The estimated standard deviations of the material control test statistics are maintained at or below a level sufficient to achieve the loss detection capabilities established pursuant to §74.53(b) without incurring an excessive rate of false alarms.

Sufficient control standard measurements and replicate analyses of process materials are performed to permit a determination of the standard deviation associated with each measured quantity.

Acceptance Criteria: Proposed mixing and sampling studies appear to be adequate for assessing the capabilities of a sampling technique to produce representative samples. Considerations applicable to sampling techniques are:

- Sample size should be a function of material homogeneity, number of containers sampled (if compositing), physical form of the material, and the sampling device used.

- Sampling of solutions containing solids should be avoided whenever possible unless it can be shown that representative sampling is possible or the solids have no SSNM content and do not contribute any significant error to the bulk volume or bulk weight measurement.

- Subsampling requirements should also be addressed in the sampling evaluations.

- Grab sampling should generally be avoided unless it can be shown that the involved materials are sufficiently homogeneous and stable.

- Sample integrity during storage can be demonstrated by a comparison of measurement results taken immediately with results on the same samples following an extended period of storage.

Calibration and control standards have assigned or certified values that are traceable through an unbroken chain of comparisons, including the overall uncertainty in each, to a national standard or physical constant.

Control standards should be representative of the material being measured with respect to matrix and SSNM concentration unless it can be demonstrated that the non-representative aspects have a negligible impact in that measurement results are unbiased.

Control measures that will ensure or confirm the continuing validity of standards' assigned values are maintained. Examples of the types of controls that would be appropriate are:

- Storage of metal standard weights in a non-corrosive atmosphere,

- Tamper-safing of NDA standards immediately after makeup,

- Storage of solution standards in more than one container when usage will be over an extended time period (e.g., 1 month),

- Storage of standards with an affinity for moisture in a desiccator, and

- Remeasurement of the standard to confirm that its value has not changed.

The alarm threshold for a material control test is adjusted when a statistically significant change of the standard deviation is indicated. The change of the standard deviation is considered significant when the null hypothesis for an F test is rejected at the 0.05 level.

Calibration procedures are adequate to ensure that the measurement systems will generate reliable results. Considerations in this regard are:

- The number of runs to establish the initial calibration is sufficient to establish a reproducible calibration.

- The calibration range spans the anticipated range of process values and standards for calibration are adequately spread over the range.

- For point calibrations utilizing a single calibration standard, the unknowns should be within $\pm 10\%$ of the assigned value of the involved standard.

Control standard measurements are spread out across the material balance period with the expressed objectives of monitoring calibrations for trends or sudden shifts and providing the necessary data for bias estimates.

Recalibrations are performed when a need is identified. Recalibrations would be deemed necessary when:

- A trend, shift, or out-of-control condition at the 0.001 level is detected;

- A bias estimate is statistically significant at the 95% confidence level;

- A change in process materials occurs that extends or shifts the needed range of calibration; or

- A change or modification is made to a measurement system that has the potential to affect measurement results.

All measurement systems affecting a material control test, ID estimate, or shipper-receiver comparison are monitored for bias except as noted below. The intensity of the monitoring program is proportional to the significance of the measurement system for the test involved. The key measurement systems (i.e., those that contribute at least 10% of the estimated measurement standard deviation of a material control test, a shipper-receiver difference, or an ID estimator) are tested for bias at least monthly except where:

- The measurement system has been demonstrated to be quite stable and the results predictable,

- The bias estimate of a measurement system utilized solely for material control test affects inputs and outputs equally and therefore the effects of bias cancel,

- The bias estimate for a measurement system utilized solely for material control test is shown to be constant and does not impact the material control test, or

- The system is defined as bias-free.

Where the above conditions exist, the bias tests can be extended to 3 months or exempted altogether if the system qualifies as bias-free.

The bias tests will be made using the mean of at least eight control standard measurements. Bias corrections will be made to individual items if the bias exceeds twice the standard deviation of its estimator and also exceeds the rounding error of affected items. Otherwise, bias corrections are applied as corrections to the ID, unless the net sum of such biases is less than 50 grams of SSNM, in which case no correction to the ID is necessary.

All other measurement systems (unless bias free) shall be monitored for bias and tested every 3 months except for those measurement systems involved with movement of material across the MAA boundary and no cross-check measurement is performed. Such systems shall also be tested monthly.

Measurement systems are considered to be "bias-free" if a representative standard is run for each unknown or set of unknowns measured at the same time, or representative standards are measured before or after a group of process samples and the standard(s) measurement response and assigned value, rather than any previous calibration information, are used in determining the value of the unknown(s).

Error variances associated with calibrations will be determined and applied in accordance with the following:

- For point calibrations, where a standard is measured with each unknown, the uncertainty associated with the standard measurement is treated as a random error, while the uncertainty associated with the standard's assigned value is treated as a fixed error.

- For point calibrations, where standards are run before and after a group of process samples and the average measured value of the standards is utilized in the element and/or isotope determination, the uncertainty associated with the standard's average measured value is treated as a fixed error for the group of process samples.

- For line or curve calibrations, the uncertainty associated with the calibration parameters is treated as a fixed error.

Correlations between terms are taken into account in the determination of fixed errors whenever bias corrections are made to calibrations.

Data from comparison programs and from intralaboratory comparisons are not acceptable for determining bias.

The methods of monitoring and controlling measurement performance are adequate to ensure the reliability of the measurement systems used for MC&A purposes. Examples of acceptable methods include control charts and automated data analysis performed on an ongoing basis. Considerations to be taken into account include:

- The proposed method is capable of providing timely information on the control status of measurement systems including the possible presence of unacceptable trends.

- The control limits are established at the 0.05 and 0.001 levels of significance or are more conservative.

- Response actions include commitments to

  1) collect additional data when a single point exceeds the 0.05 limit,

  2) notify the individual responsible for the measurement control program when two consecutive data points fall between the 0.05 and 0.001 limits,

  3) initiate an investigation to identify an assignable cause when a data point exceeds the 0.001 out-of-control limit and

  4) remove out-of-control measurement systems from service until control is reestablished at the 0.05 control limit.

4.4.2 Measurement Control for Detection/Response Measurements

Describe the specific measurement control program elements applicable to those measurement systems used for detection and response purposes. (Note: References may be made to Section 4.4.1, as appropriate.)

Affirmations:

A statistical control system is maintained to ensure that measurements employed for MC&A purposes are obtained from measurement systems that are in a state of statistical control. Control limits are established at the 0.05 and 0.001 levels of significance.

When a process modification occurs, sufficient data are generated to provide a reliable estimate of the standard deviation applicable to the material control test.

The magnitude of the uncertainties associated with process variabilities is determined and applied in the overall uncertainty (standard deviation) utilized in establishing alarm thresholds.

Acceptance Criteria: The estimated standard deviations of the material control test statistics are derived from the monitoring program data that are collected in such a manner that they represent the current performance of the process and measurement systems. Values obtained when the process is operating in an abnormal manner or when a significant process upset or anomaly has occurred will not be included in the data used to estimate the standard deviation. However, data are discarded only on the basis of preestablished objective criteria. Data may not be pooled over periods of time when significant process or measurement system changes have occurred. When data pooling is appropriate, statistical tests will be applied to demonstrate that the means and variances are from the same distribution at the 0.05 level of significance. The data will be tested for randomness (see Jaech 1977, Section 2.9-2, and Bennett and Bowen 1988) and normality when tests, such as the F-test on variances, are distribution dependent.

The quality control program for monitoring detection system effectiveness should have as its key goal assurance that the estimates of standard deviations used in establishing action thresholds that comply with the detection probability criteria neither underestimate nor overestimate the true standard deviations of the tests. It is important to ensure that the estimate of the mean and standard deviation for each material control test reflects the actual operating conditions and error sources. Generally, this is done by calculating them from sets of material control test data, but it is very important to avoid serious inflation of the variability of the data that would result in the event of actual losses of SSNM or out-of-control process variables. Therefore, both the measurement component and the overall standard deviation should be monitored for diagnostic purposes. Failure to consider all sources of noncorrectable variation, including normal process variations, would result in an unrealistically small estimate. Use of too small an estimate could result in an action threshold being set too high to provide the required loss detection probability.

The standard deviation of each material control test statistic is periodically checked by comparing an estimate of the current standard deviation with the prior value used in setting the alarm threshold. The estimate of the current standard deviation will be based on at least the 10 most recent values of a test statistic whereas the reference value will be based on at least 20 values.

4.4.3 Measurement Control for Inventory and Shipper-Receiver Measurements	Describe the measurement control program applicable to those measurement systems utilized for inventory and shipper-receiver purposes. (Note: References may be made to Section 4.4.1, as appropriate.)

Affirmations:
The cumulative shipper-receiver differences for each like material type are routinely monitored, and when, for any consecutive six-month period, they are determined to be statistically significant and exceed the larger of 1 FKG or 0.1% of the quantity received, corrective action is taken to identify and correct measurement biases.

Acceptance Criteria:
Inventory and shipper-receiver measurement systems are monitored for bias as noted in relevant acceptance criteria in Section 4.4.1 (*Common Measurement Control Practices*).

4.4.4 Standard Error of the Inventory Difference Estimator
Provide an explanation of the statistical basis for determining the SEID estimator. The description should include the means of monitoring the overall measurement system uncertainties to ensure that the SEID does not exceed the applicable limit defined in §74.59(e)(5).

In the Annex, provide the statistical model and equations or literature reference with an example calculation of a typical material balance.

Affirmations:
The methods used to estimate the SEID will be based on commonly accepted statistical principles.

Current inventory period control data are used for the estimation of the SEID and the standard deviations associated with the process differences. Data generated in immediately preceding material balance periods may be combined with current data when it can be demonstrated that the data are from the same distribution, and the combined data are utilized to establish current period measurement uncertainty values.

Measurement system performance is controlled such that the total SEID will not exceed 0.1% of the active inventory.

Acceptance Criteria:
The measurement control program produces data that are representative of actual operating conditions and all errors that impact ID. The larger uncertainty estimates that collectively contribute 90 percent or more to the standard error of the ID estimator will be based on a minimum of 15 standard or replicate process material measurements, as appropriate.

The licensee has demonstrated that the SEID estimator meets the requirement of §74.59(e)(5).

The method to be used for estimating the SEID for the typical material balance, as shown in the Annex, meets the following criteria:

- All reasonable and probable sources of measurement error for the key measurement systems affecting IDs are included.

- The selection of the key measurements whose variances are to be included in calculating the standard error is justified by an analysis of the relative magnitudes of the variance components of a typical ID and their comparative effect on the SEID.

- Any measurement error standard deviations not actually determined by the measurement control program are shown to be reasonable either by comparison with published state-of-the-art measurement performance in similar applications: (see such sources as Rogers [1983], and Reilly and Evans [1977]) or with records of past performance data from the licensee's facility. Records showing these data must be available to the NRC.

- The calculation of the SEID is performed in accordance with a recognized error propagation method. Such methods have been published by Jaech (1973), and the IAEA (1977).

4.4.5 Cumulative Shipper-Receiver Differences

Describe the program for monitoring cumulative shipper-receiver differences (CUMSRDs). The description should include:

- The means of determining the uncertainty against which the significance of the difference will be assessed; and

- The course of action with respect to review of measurement systems, shipper notification, and treatment with respect to impact on ID (i.e., how the impact of the CUMSRD will be accounted for in the evaluation of ID significance).

Affirmations:

The methods used to evaluate the CUMSRDs will be based on commonly accepted statistical principles.

Acceptance Criteria:

CUMSRDs on like kinds of material (derived from the same measurement system) will be monitored for trends that may be indicative of a bias in the shipper's or receiver's measurements. For the purpose of this requirement, "like kinds of material" means major categories having the same chemical and physical form (e.g., UF_6, PuO_2 powder, UC coated particles, etc.).

The standard deviation applicable to a shipper-receiver difference should take into account all measurement variance and covariance effects. The CUMSRD should be evaluated and tested at least once every month, and pursuant to §74.59(e)(7), investigative and corrective actions (as applicable) shall be taken whenever the CUMSRD for any consecutive six-month period (even if not statistically significant) is greater than the larger of 1.000 FKG or 0.10 percent of the total amount of SSNM received during the six-month period in question. Appropriate statistical methodology for analyzing CUMSRDs can be found in Rose and Scholz (1983).

4.5 Physical Inventory [§74.59(f)]

Requirements

Unless required otherwise by a procedure commitment made pursuant to 10 CFR 75.21(b)(4), perform a physical inventory at least every 6 calendar months and within 45 days from the ending inventory date;

- Calculate the inventory difference, estimate the standard error of difference, and investigate and report any SEID estimate of 0.10 percent or more of active inventory and any inventory difference that exceeds three times the standard error and 200 grams of plutonium or 233-uranium or 300 grams of 235-uranium;

- If required to perform an ID investigation pursuant to §74.59(f)(1)(i), evaluate the significance of the inventory difference relative to expected ID performance as determined from an analysis of an appropriate sequence of historical inventory differences;

- Investigate and report to the appropriate NRC safeguards licensing authority any inventory difference that exceeds three times the standard deviation determined from the sequential analysis;

- Perform a reinventory if so directed by NRC; and

- Reconcile and adjust the plant and subsidiary book inventories to the results of the physical inventory.

Implement policies and procedures designed to ensure the quality of physical inventories. Appropriate practices and procedures shall include:

- Procedures for tamper-safing containers or vaults containing SSNM not in process that include adequate controls to ensure the validity of assigned SSNM values,

- Records of the quantities of SSNM added to and removed from process,

- Requirements for signed documentation of all SSNM transfer between areas with different custodial responsibility that reflects all quantities of SSNM transferred,

- Means for control of and accounting for internal transfer documents,

- Cutoff procedures for transfers and processing so that all quantities are inventoried and none are inventoried more than once,

- Cutoff procedures for records and reports so that all transfers for the inventory and material balance interval and no others are included in the records,

- Inventory procedures for sealed sources and containers or vaults containing SSNM that ensure reliable identification and quantification of contained SSNM,

- Inventory procedures for in-process SSNM that provide for measurement of quantities not previously measured for element and isotope, as appropriate, and remeasurement of material previously measured but whose validity has not been ensured by tamper-safing or encapsulation, and

- Written instructions for conducting physical inventories that detail assignments, responsibilities, preparation, and performance of inventory.

Intent and Scope   Periodic physical inventories enable a licensee to adjust accounts to accurately reflect the status of the SSNM inventory within a facility. Comparisons of the book inventory to the physical inventory (i.e., the inventory difference) also serve as a quality control check on the performance of the material control tests employed for prompt loss detection. The subdivision of a facility into multiple process units and the performance of material control tests will enhance the resolution of significant IDs through better loss localization capability. Additionally, material control test results will be useful in pinpointing the time when an anomaly likely occurred.

4.5.1 Facility Preparation   Describe the preparation of the facility for physical inventory. The description should include:

- The basic approach to facility preparation (e.g., draindown, cleanout, etc.),

- The degree to which any inventory prelisting will be utilized, and the means of verifying the prelisted items,

- The means of controlling inventory listing forms and tags,

- The cutoff procedures for SSNM processing, transfers, and records adjustments to ensure an accurate recording of material transactions and inventory listing,

- The organization of the inventory teams including the cross-checks to prevent falsification and minimize mistakes, and

- The criteria, controls, and procedures for tamper-safing containers or vaults whose SSNM content (as established by prior measurement) will be accepted for inventory.

Affirmations: Measures are taken to prepare a facility for the physical inventory to ensure adequate preparation by the cutoff deadline and to minimize the occurrence of inventory listing errors.

Acceptance Criteria: The physical inventory procedures provide for verifying the location and identity of all quantities of SSNM. The SSNM quantity of each component in the material balance is based on measurements. "By difference accounting", is not acceptable.

4.5.2 Inventory Performance

Describe how physical inventories are conducted. The description should address the following:

- The technique to ensure that all SSNM is inventoried and none is counted more than once,

- The measurements that will be performed specifically for inventory purposes,

- The use of prior measurement data, factors, and composite data,

- The degree to which process holdup will be cleaned out and the measurement of residual holdup, and

- The use of post-inventory inspection techniques (if employed).

In the Annex provide an example of a typical inventory listing by material type and quantity.

Affirmations: A measured physical inventory is performed every 6 calendar months and within 45 days of the start of the ending inventory:

- An ID and the associated standard error are calculated.

- Any SEID that equals or exceeds 0.10 percent of active inventory, and any ID greater than 300 grams of 235-uranium (200 grams of plutonium or 233-uranium) and three times the SEID is reported to the NRC and investigated.

- All investigations associated with IDs that exceed both three times SEID and 300 grams 235-uranium (200 grams plutonium or 233-uranium) include an evaluation of the significance of the ID relative to expected performance as determined from an analysis of an appropriate sequence of historical inventory differences.

- Any inventory difference that exceeds three times the standard deviation of historical IDs as determined from the sequential analysis is investigated and reported to the appropriate NRC safeguards licensing authority.

NOTE: Actions in response to excessive IDs are to be described in Section 4.5.3 (*Inventory Reconciliation*).

Acceptance Criteria: Inventory cutoff and cutoff verification procedures, tag procedures, and post-inventory inspections or equally effective measures are used to ensure all quantities are accounted for and not counted more than once. Sufficient information is provided in the plan to show that the inventory process is organized and coordinated to ensure the use of uniform and consistent procedures for checking and recording the SSNM status.

The SSNM content of groups of like items can be determined by averaging typical contents as determined by measurements of representative item samples of that material at the time of the inventory if the licensee demonstrates that any additional uncertainty resulting from this averaging method is included in the SEID estimator.

With respect to the processing of scrap generated in a prior period, the current period assigned value must be based on dissolver solution and dissolver residue measurements, and not on the product of the scrap plant. This is because losses may occur during the separation and purification stage which should, in fact, be attributable to current period processing. Any difference between the prior period value and the value obtained from after dissolution plus residue measurements is to be treated as a prior period adjustment to the ID for the current period.

All SSNM values on the physical inventory listing must be based on measurements. Prior measurement values may be accepted for inventory provided they were determined on a measurement system subject to the licensee's measurement control program, and the containers were either tamper-safed, stored in an area that provided protection equivalent to tamper-safing, or encapsulated. Otherwise, the previously measured SSNM content of items on ending inventory must be verified by remeasurement.

4.5.3 Inventory Reconciliation

Describe the reconciliation procedure including:

* The method of calculating the SEID,

* The criteria for investigation of IDs that exceed three times the SEID and also exceed 200 grams of plutonium or U-233 or 300 grams U-235,

* The method of establishing 3 times the standard deviation of historical IDs against which an ID that exceeds 3 times the SEID will be evaluated,

* The criteria for establishing the depth of investigation for excessive IDs and the types of investigative actions,

* The handling of prior period adjustments and measurement system biases that are applied as corrections to an ID,

* The method of adjusting the book records to the results of the physical inventory, and

* The means of establishing the active inventory including the source records that will be used in the computation.

Affirmations: The material accounting records are reconciled and adjusted to the results of the physical inventory.

Acceptance Criteria: Adjustments to reconcile the book inventory to the physical inventory will be in accordance with commonly accepted accounting practices, and the adjustments will be traceable and auditable.

The effect of prior period adjustments will be taken into account before the significance of the current period ID is assessed. Prior period adjustments could be the result of:

* Corrections of a recording or measurement error associated with material on beginning inventory (BI),

- Resolution within the current period of a statistically significant shipper-receiver difference involving material that was on BI, or

- An adjustment to the initial receipt value pertaining to scrap, received in a prior period, due to better measurement following dissolution of such scrap in the current period.

The appropriate procedures for dealing with biases not applied to individual items and for prior period adjustments is, for purposes of ID evaluation, to modify the ID quantity by adding or subtracting a quantity of SSNM equivalent to the net total of adjustments so as to obtain an adjusted ID that reflects the current period ID. ID bias corrections and prior period adjustments are not, however, applied as adjustments to the book inventory value.

Assessment of the significance of current period material balance results by sequential analysis of prior period ID data, as required by § 74.59(f)(1)(ii) whenever ID exceeds 3 times SEID, requires consideration of several relevant points. These are:

- The sequence of IDs used for analysis should possess essentially the same components as the current period. That is, the throughputs should be approximately the same (e.g., within ± 25%), the same process units should be operational, and the process should not have undergone any major modifications. With respect to the unit operations, it is not essential that all units operate every period but rather that the grouping of IDs for analysis take into account which units were operative. As to process modifications, a major modification would be one that has a significant impact on measurement capabilities or holdup patterns. "Significant" means a change in the SEID of ± 30% or greater.

- The analysis of a sequence of IDs to establish a representative standard deviation must take into account the covariances that exist between adjacent (lag 1) and alternate (lag 2) pairs. The AAMASS methodology (Lumb and Tingey 1981) and INDEP (Lumb and Associates 1986) provide two acceptable means of determining the historical standard deviations taking covariances into account.

The criteria against which the significance of a current period ID should be evaluated can be established by at least two different methods. These are:

- Control chart limits constructed with current and historical material balance closure data, where such limits for further action should be established at a level of significance of 0.01. The limits should be based on the statistical variance-covariance structure of the current inventory difference and an appropriate sequence of previous inventory differences; or

- Three sigma control limits where sigma is determined as described in Section 4.4.4 (*Standard Error of the Inventory Difference Estimator*) for SEID.

Excessive IDs must be investigated and appropriate action taken. The following are actions that would be deemed appropriate:

- If ID > 3 times SEID and 300 grams 235-uranium (200 grams plutonium or 233-uranium):

  1) Review inventory listing to ensure that all items and item quantities have been listed, and none listed more than once.

  2) Review measurement results for previously unidentified biases.

  3) Review inventory documentation and book records for human errors and make appropriate corrections.

  4) Review inventory documentation and book records for anomalies, and investigate any anomalies to determine any need for remeasurements.

  5) Review holdup estimates for reasonableness relative to historical data.

  6) Calculate a standard deviation (σ_{ID}) representative of relevant historical ID performance.

- If ID < 3 times σ_{ID}, no additional investigative actions needed.

- If 5 FKG > ID > 3 σ_{ID}:

  1) Compare material control test and item monitoring data with results of the physical inventory.

  2) Review results of trends analyses for all process units.

  3) Review conclusions of alarm investigations.

- If 10 FKG > ID > 3 σ_{ID} and 5 FKG

  1) Same as above, and

  2) Review plant security records.

  3) Conduct next inventory within 2 months or as directed by NRC.

- If ID > 3 σ_{ID} and > 10 FKG:

  1) Same as above.

  2) Prepare facility for an immediate reinventory.

  3) Remeasure a statistically determined sample of the items on hand at ending inventory for the material balance period in question that is sufficient to detect, with a 99% probability, at least one defective item if an actual loss of 5 or more FKG from the ending inventory quantity occurred. A defective item is one that has had some or all of its SSNM contents removed, and the quantity removed exceeds 3 times the combined standard error of measurement (when taking into account the measurement uncertainties of both the original measurement and the remeasurement)

  4) For shipments (other than waste) made during the period, contact the appropriate receivers and request S/R evaluation data. For those shipments not yet measured by the receiver, request immediate measurement and resulting S/R evaluation data. Review all S/R data for the period for possible biases, measurement errors, and loss indications.

The concept of active inventory is adequately described and represents the quantity of material typically handled under normal plant operating conditions.

Questions and Answers:

Q What is the distinction between an ID estimate and estimator?

A Because of unavoidable uncertainties in any measurement, the true amount of material being measured is unknown. The measurement can be considered to be a random variable characterized by a probability distribution. As a random variable, the measurement process is referred to in statistical terminology as an estimator. A particular value realized by

79

applying an estimator is referred to as an estimate. Since ID is a function of measured values, it is sometimes useful to distinguish between true ID, its estimator, and a single estimate. The ID calculated at the end of an inventory is a point estimate. There is no guarantee, in fact it is highly unlikely, that the ID estimate will exactly equal the true ID. The ID estimator random variable can be written as:

$$ID = BI + A - EI - R,$$

where ending inventory (EI), beginning inventory (BI), additions (A) and removals (R) are also random variables. In this form of the ID equation, the inventory terms must represent all inventory including residual holdup.

Q Why not use limit of error as the measure of ID variability?

A Although the limit of error of ID (LEID) has been used for some time in nuclear material accounting, the terminology is a departure from statistical terminology taught in schools and universities, and as a result, it has been the source of some confusion. In practice LEID has been calculated as twice the standard deviation of the measurement error associated with the ID. It should be realized that licensees need only use an estimate for the standard deviation.

Q How does the constraint on measurement system quality (i.e., 0.1% of active inventory) compare to the LEID limit in 10 CFR 70.51?

A The LEID limit for most processes is 0.5% of the throughput, which is the larger of additions to or removals from process. Since active inventory, which replaces throughput because it is a more widely applicable measure of the amount of material subject to measurement error in an inventory period, involves the sum of additions and removals, it is approximately double throughput. Thus, the LEID limit could be expressed as "approximately 0.25% of active inventory." The LEID is also 2 times the standard deviation of ID (measurement component only). Thus the LEID limit can be expressed as "2 times the standard deviation must be less than 0.25% of active inventory." This equates to 1 standard deviation (or SEID) being less than 0.125% of active inventory. The limit for SEID under §74.59(e)(5) is 0.100% of active inventory since measurement equipment is better than it was when the LEID limit of 0.5% throughput was originally imposed in the 1970's.

4.6 Accounting [§74.59(g)]

Requirements

The rule requires that a licensee establish auditable records sufficient to demonstrate that the requirements of §74.53, §74.55, §74.57, and §74.59 have been met. The records are to be retained for at least 3 years or longer if required by 10 CFR Part 75.

Intent and Scope

The intent of these requirements is that the licensee establish an auditable records system that contains sufficient information to facilitate future reviews, audits, and inspections to demonstrate that all Plan commitments have been met. As a minimum, the records system should include data and information on material control tests; item monitoring; alarm resolution; SSNM receipts, shipments, and discards; measurement control; physical inventories; and MC&A program assessments.

4.6.1 Records System

Provide a general description of the records system including recordkeeping policies and the types of data and information routinely recorded. The types of records to be retained and their form should also be described.

In the Annex, provide flow charts showing the flow of data from the source documents to the final accounting records and the typical forms and report formats used throughout the MC&A system.

Affirmations:

A records system is maintained that contains auditable records sufficient to demonstrate compliance with all commitments reflected in this Plan.

Acceptance Criteria:

The records system provides for retention of key material accounting and original source data and relevant reports and documents including:

- Management structure,

- MC&A policies and procedures,

- Measurement data used for loss detection, alarm resolution, and material balance accounting,

- Records of the investigation and resolution of alarms,

- Calibrations of measurement systems, measurement quality control data, bias adjustments and their backup data, and the statistical analyses of the measurement control data,

- Calculations of action thresholds for the detection system,

- Shipper/receiver data and investigations of significant shipper/receiver differences,

- Tamper-safing records (e.g., application records, "attesting to" records, destruction records),

- Physical inventory listings and inventory work sheets,

- Records of IDs and calculations of the SEIDs,

- Reports of investigations and resolution of alarms, excessive ID estimates, and shipper/receiver differences, and

- Reports of periodic reviews and assessments of MC&A program elements and the resultant corrective actions taken by management.

Records may be retained in hard copy, magnetic tapes or disks, microfiche, or other suitable forms.

The records and reports contain sufficient detail to enable inspectors to determine that SSNM control and accounting have been conducted in compliance with §74.53, §74.55, §74.57 and §74.59.

The record system will be complete and sufficiently detailed to permit auditing of all parts of the MC&A system. The records and reports will be readily traceable back to source documents.

The types of data and information routinely recorded and maintained in the records system for SSNM includes:

- Identification (numeric or alpha-numeric),

- Date of generation/creation and name of operator(s),

- Date of measurement(s) and name of individual(s) performing measurement(s),

- Measurement method(s),

- Measurement value(s),

- Location,

- Name of individuals applying tamper-safe seal and seal number, if used.

4.6.2 Record Maintenance

Describe the measures that will be taken to ensure record integrity including:

- Physical protection,

- Assignment of overall responsibility,

- Access controls which permit only authorized updating and correcting of records,

- Cross-checks for preventing or detecting missing or falsified data and records, ensuring completeness of the records, and locating data discrepancies and errors, and

- Capability for reconstructing lost or destroyed records.

Affirmations:

Sufficient protection and redundancy of the record system are provided so that an act of record alteration or destruction will not eliminate the capability to provide a complete and correct set of SSNM control and accounting information that could be used to detect the loss of a goal quantity or more, resolve indications of missing material, or aid in the investigation and recovery of missing material.

Controls are incorporated in the records system to maximize the likelihood that mistakes and attempts at data falsification will be detected.

SSNM transactions are traceable from source data to the final accounting records.

Acceptance Criteria:

The record system will have sufficient redundancy to enable reconstruction of lost or missing records so that a complete knowledge of the SSNM inventory is available. The capability for reconstruction of records will be provided by a sub-system at least equivalent to the following: source data for receipts, shipments, internal transfers, adjustments, and corrections to the records will be retained in a separate secure location so that a single individual or a single event cannot alter both accounting and source records.

Cross-checks or other controls will be provided to prevent or detect errors in the records that would affect IDs or item location records. Examples of cross-checks or controls that might prevent or detect errors in the records system would include:

- Minimizing the number of people authorized to make data entries,

83

- Use of card readers and passwords (or equivalent controls) to preclude unauthorized data entries,

- Using verification methods for data entry for shipments, receipts, waste discards, and item records (item records may be checked by random sampling rather than on a 100% basis), and

- cross-checking calculations, at least by random sampling.

The records of the data that are the basis of the SEID will permit traceability to the sources of the variances due to calibrations, bias adjustments, and random errors in the measurements. These records may simply be summaries of calibrations, bias tests, and variance monitoring data or control charts.

Records less than 1 year old can be retrieved within 24 hours and records older than 1 year with 7 calendar days.

4.7 Shipments and Receipts [§74.59(h)(1)]

Requirement   The rule requires that a licensee shall establish procedures for shipping and receiving SNM that provide for:

- Accurate identification and measurement of the quantities shipped and received,

- Review and evaluation of shipper/receiver differences on an individual container or batch (lot) basis, and on a shipment basis,

- Investigation and corrective action when shipper/receiver differences exceed twice the estimated standard deviation of the difference estimator and the larger of 0.5% of the amount of SSNM in the container, lot, or shipment, as appropriate, or 50 grams of SSNM,

- Documentation of shipper/receiver evaluations, investigations and corrective actions.

Intent and Scope   Timely and accurate quantification of the SSNM content of shipments and receipts is an essential component of an effective MC&A system. When significant shipper/receiver differences are identified, it is imperative that they be resolved and contributing factors corrected.

4.7.1 Receiving Procedure

Describe how materials are received, stored, and measured. The latter should include a description of the sampling techniques employed.

Affirmations:

Receipts of SSNM are checked and measured to confirm that the quantity received is consistent with the shipper's supporting documentation. Item checks and seal integrity inspections are completed within 24 hours of receipt. Receipt measurements are completed within 30 days of receipt except in the case of scrap.

Acceptance Criteria:

Receipts are inspected promptly to verify the validity of the shipper's data. Acceptable times to complete the verifications measures are:

- Item verification, 24 hours,

- Seal integrity, 24 hours,

- Gross weight, 72 hours,

- NDA measurements (if appropriate), 120 hours, and

- Destructive measurements (scrap excepted), 30 days.

Times other than those indicated above would be acceptable with adequate justification.

Shipper's values may be accepted and booked without receiver verification measurements for encapsulated items such as fuel rods, elements, etc. if an NDA measurement is not feasible. However, an exemption from §74.59(d)(1) would be necessary.

4.7.2 Shipper-Receiver Differences

Describe the investigation of significant shipper-receiver differences. The description should include:

- The method of establishing the standard deviation of the shipper-receiver difference estimator under conditions when the shipper's uncertainty estimate is available and also when it is unavailable,

- The conditions under which a referee laboratory is involved and the criteria for selecting a referee laboratory,

- The bases established for concluding that a significant difference is resolved,

- The procedure for adjusting book records to accommodate resolution of the difference, and

• The procedure for establishing and resolving differences involving scrap.

Affirmations:

Shipper/receiver differences are investigated whenever they exceed twice the standard deviation of the difference estimator and the larger of 0.5% of the amount of SSNM in the container, lot or shipment, as appropriate, or 50 grams of SSNM.

Results of shipper/receiver difference investigations, including corrective actions, are documented and retained for at least 3 years.

Acceptance Criteria:

The investigation of statistically significant shipper-receiver differences should normally be completed within 3 months except where the difference exceeds 5 FKG. In the latter case, the discrepancy should be resolved within 30 days of the time that its existence is determined.

The NRC is to be notified of any inability to resolve any statistically significant S/R difference that exceeds the larger of 50 grams SSNM or 0.50 % of the SSNM quantity involved. Such notification is to be made within 30 days following the receipt of the material for differences that equal or exceed 5 FKG, and within 90 days for differences that are less than 5 FKG.

The following stepwise analysis is an example of an acceptable approach for investigating a significant shipper-receiver difference:

• The receiver reviews its data to check for possible entry errors such as an incorrect number or the transposition of numbers.

• The receiver then reviews source data including the basic calculations and the associated measurement control data.

• Assuming the difference remains unresolved, the receiver remeasures the SSNM content of the receipt.

• If remeasurement fails to resolve the difference, the shipper is notified and requested to conduct a similar investigation.

• If the two parties fail to resolve the difference, a referee laboratory should be involved. The shipper and receiver should mutually agree on the sampling procedure.

• Unless contractual requirements dictate otherwise, the value closest to the referee's value is accepted and booked by both parties. If the referee's value is not within statistical limits of either the shipper or receiver, but lies between the two, the referee's value is used.

For purposes of shipper-receiver evaluation, a "lot" may be defined in several ways. These would include:

- Multiple containers of a material that has been blended by a procedure that has been demonstrated to produce a homogeneous product,

- Multiple containers filled from a master container of homogeneous material (e.g., UF6 cylinders),

- A quantity of scrap transferred on multiple transfer receipts (DOE/NRC Form 741) but combined for processing through recovery.

4.7.3 Shipping Procedure

Describe the preparation and certification procedures for shipping SSNM. The description should include:

- The measurement data and tamper-safing information provided to the group responsible for SSNM shipments,

- The cross-checks, including any item checks or measurements, made by the shipping group, and

- The types of records maintained by the shipping group.

Affirmations:

The element and isotopic content of SSNM shipped by the licensee are based on measurements obtained from measurement systems subject to the measurement control program.

Acceptance Criteria:

The documentation of shipments and receipts should be completed and transmitted within the time specified in NUREG/BR-0006.

Only acceptable tamper-safing methods will be used as described in Section 2.1.3 (*Tamper-safing*) and as agreed to with the receiver.

4.8 Scrap Control [§74.59(h)(2)]

Requirement

The rule requires that a licensee establish a scrap control program that ensures that internally generated scrap is segregated from scrap from other licensees or contractors until accountability is established, and any scrap with a measurement standard deviation greater than 5% of the measured amount is recovered so that the results are segregated by inventory period and recovered within 6 months of the end of the inventory period in which the scrap was generated except where it can be demonstrated that the scrap measurement uncertainty will not cause noncompliance with §74.59(e)(5).

Intent and Scope
The regular processing of scrap with relatively large measurement uncertainties precludes such scrap being the source of a problem at the time of physical inventories. Inaccurate scrap measurements could cause an apparent ID or conceal a theft or diversion. Segregation of internally generated scrap from that received from off-site until accountability is established ensures that potential anomalies in assigned values will be attributed to the appropriate facility.

4.8.1 Location

Identify the scrap and waste quantities of contained SSNM with respect to source, storage, and disposition. Refer to process flow charts and plant operations descriptions included in the Annex.

Affirmations:
Scrap and waste will only be stored in approved locations and disposal of by approved methods.

Acceptance Criteria:
Storage locations for scrap and waste are identified. Scrap and waste generation rates are estimated for each process unit. Methods for disposition of waste are described.

4.8.2 Processing

Describe the program for in-house processing of scrap including recovery plant capacity, rate of recovery, and the estimated amount of scrap expected to be on hand at any given time. Describe any plans for shipments and for off-site recovery of scrap. Describe procedures for the control and discard of wastes containing SSNM, including procedures and capabilities for storage prior to discard.

Affirmations:
Adequate onsite recovery capacity and/or adequate provision for offsite recovery exist to ensure compliance with the requirements of §74.59(e)(5).

Acceptance Criteria:
A comparison of generation rates and recovery capacity indicates that adequate recovery capability exists to preclude the buildup of excess amounts of scrap.

4.8.3 Measurements

Describe the procedures for determining the SSNM content of scrap and waste, including the criteria and procedures for segregation, identification, and classification of various kinds of scrap to facilitate measurement. Identify types and quantities of scrap expected to have measurement uncertainties greater than $\pm 5\%$ (1σ).

Affirmations: Listed quantities of scrap and waste present during a physical inventory will be derived from measurements when possible. Otherwise, such SSNM quantities will be based on average historical factors, which in turn are derived from measurements performed on each type of scrap and waste in question.

Methods used to measure scrap and waste are subject to the measurement control program described in Section 4.4.1 (*Common Measurement Control Practices*).

Acceptance Criteria: Special handling procedures for waste such as conversion to a better measurable form or independent measurement verification are described.

Proposed measurement techniques for specific scrap types are described including the following where appropriate:

- Material description,

- Specific NDA system to be employed,

- Container size,

- Mixing and blending operations,

- Sampling technique, and

- Assay procedure.

An estimate of the measurement uncertainties associated with each scrap type is included in the Annex.

For those materials measured by NDA in 30-gallon drums or larger containers, the licensee should commit to an annual evaluation to demonstrate the continuing reliability of the measurement system. Possible evaluation techniques include a destructive analysis, a second NDA technique not subject to the same potential interferences as the primary technique, or a standard addition procedure.

4.8.4 Inventory Control   Describe the control program that will be implemented to ensure that scrap measured with a measurement standard deviation greater than $\pm$ 5% does not remain on inventory longer than 6 months beyond the inventory period in which it was generated, or that the measurement uncertainty associated with the scrap on hand will not cause noncompliance with §74.59(e)(5).

Affirmations: Scrap control procedures are in place that provide for recovery of scrap within 6 months after the inventory period in which it was generated, when such scrap has a standard deviation of its measurement estimator greater than 5% of the measured amount unless it can be shown that the total scrap measurement error will not cause noncompliance with §74.59(e)(5).

Acceptance Criteria: The program for segregation of scrap generated off-site from on-site scrap appears adequate to protect against commingling. Possible techniques to achieve this objective are:

- Retain customer scrap in shipping containers prior to recovery,

- Isolate customer scrap in a particular section of a vault or permanently controlled access area, or

- Identify designated storage bins or shelves for application of limited access controls.

4.8.5 Recovery of Off-Site Scrap

Describe the procedures that will be implemented to ensure that scrap received for recovery from off-site is segregated until accountability is established. The description should address segregation during storage and processing.

Affirmations: Scrap control procedures are in place that provide for (1) segregation of scrap receipts (from off-site) from each other and from on-site generated scrap until accountability and shipper-receiver differences have been established, and (2) segregation of on-site generated scrap by plant (when a licensee has more than one on-site plant) until "after dissolution plus residue" measurements are obtained.

Acceptance Criteria: Where off-site recovery is utilized, the description of the program includes as a minimum:

- Types and estimated quantities of scrap to be shipped,

- Contractor's program to ensure segregation of customer scrap,

- Basis for establishing accountability values,

- Contractor and shipper measurement responsibilities, and

- Means of performing shipper/receiver comparisons.

Segregation of customer scrap during processing is accomplished by cleaning the dissolver and accountability weigh tank before and after the recovery campaign. Additional processing of dissolver residues should be handled in the same manner unless the quantity involved is less than 1 FKG or the measurement uncertainty is less than $\pm 5\%$ at the one σ level.

4.9. Human Errors [§74.59(h)(3)]

Requirement

The rule requires that a licensee incorporate checks and balances in the MC&A system to control the rate of human errors in MC&A information.

Intent and Scope

The objective of this requirement is to reduce the frequency of human errors affecting MC&A information and to enhance the likelihood of detection when they do occur. This can be achieved by a system of checks and balances in MC&A information systems that involve generating, collecting, processing, computing, analyzing, summarizing, and reporting data.

4.9.1 MC&A Procedures

Describe the MC&A procedures developed to perform MC&A tasks, the features of these procedures that contribute to minimizing human errors in MC&A data, and the control methods used to ensure that current procedures are in place and are being used appropriately. Control methods may include maintenance of a list of procedures, periodic review by operators and during audits, use of sign off cover sheets, and validation during training sessions. The FNMCP should describe where procedures are available for subsequent monitoring during NRC inspections.

Affirmations:

MC&A procedures are developed and implemented in a manner that ensures that the frequency and consequences of human errors will be minimized.

MC&A procedures are formatted in a manner that facilitates a reduction in human errors and helps make errors easier to identify.

Acceptance Criteria:

Procedures have been developed and are used that will control the rate of human error in MC&A data.

- Specific procedures are available to guide personnel in performing major or complex tasks associated with MC&A.

- Procedures are sufficiently explicit and comprehensive to promote error-free performance by the least skilled or least experienced person that will be assigned to perform the tasks specified by the procedures.

- Procedures are based on the activities required to effectively accomplish the task.

- Procedures are self-contained to avoid the need to refer to supporting documents.

- Procedures are written with flexibility in the sequence of events whenever possible.

- Knowledgeable personnel prepare and review procedures before they are implemented.

- Lengthy and/or complex procedures are validated by means of field tests to ensure their clarity, comprehensiveness, and effectiveness.

- Personnel are required to use and follow appropriate procedures in performing complex MC&A tasks or tasks that affect MC&A.

The format of MC&A procedures is arranged to help to reduce the rate of human error and to detect mistakes.

- The complexity, sentence length, and grammatical structure are appropriate to the educational level of the least qualified user.

- Short sentences with concise and unambiguous language are used.

- The level of detail in instructions is adequate to avoid errors of omission.

- No more than three simple task elements are included per step. More complex actions are separated into additional steps.

- Procedures are formatted to allow experienced personnel to concentrate on major headings or capsule descriptions, while more detail is provided in clearly demarcated fashion for less experienced personnel. Procedures may be formatted in "cookbook" fashion for ease of use when appropriate.

- All steps and tasks are stated as actions. The sequence of steps and tasks in a procedure is in the same sequence followed to accomplish the objective of the procedure.

- Attention-getting warning and precaution notices are placed immediately preceding applicable steps and, where required, are also summarized at the beginning of the procedure.

- Summary information is included at the beginning of every procedure. All required supplies, tools, test equipment, documents, and protective measures are listed at the beginning of the procedure.

- All applicable referenced documents are listed in one section of the procedure.

- Quality control and quality assurance points are identified.

- Decision-making cues are clearly stated.

- Sub-tasks and sub-tests are set off with separate headings or by an appropriate indentation.

- The sequence of steps is logical and accurate.

- Unnecessary memory recall is avoided.

- The need for personnel to perform calculations and conversions is avoided whenever possible.

- Data collection tables and data reduction aids are provided if lengthy tests and calculations cannot be avoided.

- Pre-printed forms for recording data are utilized when practical.

- Multiple copies of forms, if needed, are generated automatically in the data collection phase.

- Formatting is neat and simple and is consistent among all related procedures.

Questions and Answers:
Q Why should there be no more than three actions per step in a procedure?

A By restricting the amount of information that personnel are required to remember while performing a procedure, there is a greater probability that the procedure will be performed correctly. Remembering precise, numerical information is

93

not a task that humans perform well. Using checklists or preprinted forms are methods to limit the amount of memorization required while reducing dependence on often bulky procedures.

Q What is configuration control and how is it applied to procedures?

A Configuration control is a method by which the current official copies of procedures are maintained and controlled. Procedures that may be used in configuration control include sign offs by a responsible person on the released version, numbering and dating versions, and periodic checks of the individual procedures under the control of the procedure custodian or holder to make sure that current copies are being used.

4.9.2 Job Performance Aids

Describe the job performance aids to be utilized for highly complex MC&A tasks to control the rate of human error in MC&A data.

Affirmations:

MC&A procedures include job performance aids, where applicable, that help to reduce the frequency of human errors.

Acceptance Criteria:

Job performance aids are provided for complex MC&A tasks.

- Job performance aids assist novice users in their performance while not hindering the performance of experienced users.

- Terms and labels match common usage for equipment labels and legends.

- Quantities and dimensional units correspond to referenced displays, documents, and information.

- Uncommon and inconsistent abbreviations are avoided.

- The presentation of illustrations, graphs, and tables, if used, is consistent throughout the procedure.

- Checklists or data tables are provided for lengthy prerequisites, tests, and calculations.

- Illustrations are used in place of long descriptions where possible.

- Illustrations are placed so that they can be referenced easily from the text section.

- Illustrations are clearly labeled and easy to read.

- All tables and graphs are clearly labeled in quantitative terms.

Questions and Answers:

Q What are some successfully used job performance aids?

A Several job performance aids (JPA) are illustrations and diagrams, graphs for interpolation, approximate times to complete specific jobs, clearly stated decision-making cues and clues to the correct decision given specific cues, and data reduction aids. JPAs are good as long as they do not cause the procedure to become difficult to use because of too many aids, the wrong types of aids, or presentation in an inappropriate manner. If the procedure can be written so that an experienced user can omit unnecessary aids meant for novice users, that in itself is a JPA and will encourage procedure usage.

Q Some of the notation and labels used on equipment at specific facilities may not be current with respect to recommended terminology. Should procedures use current terminology, or be consistent with the equipment?

A Ideally, equipment should be brought into compliance with the current idea of "best" notation on labels and panels. However, confusion could occur because personnel at the facility are accustomed to that terminology, so these labels probably should not be changed. In any case, procedure terminology should be consistent with equipment, as should forms and other information to be employed by personnel at the facility.

4.9.3 *Automation of MC&A*

Describe the methods and technologies used to automate MC&A functions and the features of these methods that contribute to minimizing human errors in MC&A data.

Affirmations:

MC&A activities associated with collecting and processing data, recordkeeping, and auditing are automated where it is practical and advantageous to do so.

Acceptance Criteria:

MC&A data are directly collected, inputted, checked, manipulated, reported and audited by computer where it is practical and advantageous to reduce the consequences and frequency of human error in MC&A data as much as practical.

*4.9.4 Human Error Quality
     Control*

Describe the quality control system that will be used to monitor the frequency and types of human errors.

Describe the techniques that will be employed to minimize the frequency and consequences of human errors and enhance the likelihood that they will be detected when they do occur. The description should address the use of:

- Control methods to ensure that current procedures are in place and being used,

- Job performance aids,

- Automated data processing,

- Personnel training and qualification,

- Preprinted forms,

- Multiple copy forms, and

- Data verification.

Affirmations: A quality control system is in place to monitor the frequency of human errors and permit categorization of the types of errors encountered.

Acceptance Criteria: Statistical quality control systems are used to track the effectiveness of human error control measures and the frequency of human error in MC&A systems, and should be used to alert management whenever the rate of human error is in an out-of-tolerance condition.

- The quality control system is capable of determining if and when an individual, procedure, or process makes more errors than is reasonably expected.

- The quality control system is capable of determining both (1) the individuals who require retraining due to their frequency of committing errors and (2) the procedures and processes that should be revised to produce fewer human errors.

- Double checklists are provided to allow periodic, random auditing of data collection by a supervisor or other independent person that checks the results of the first person's work and signs off when the work is complete and accurate. Each data collection form should be checked by the originator to verify that the data are accurate.

- When MC&A data processing is automated, quality control systems are also automated, so that out-of-tolerance conditions, human errors, and other warnings can be detected promptly.

- A configuration management plan is established for vital MC&A equipment, computer software, and manuals.

- Configuration control measures are performed systematically and immediately reflect all changes as they are made.

- Procedures and technical manuals are stored, indexed, filed, and controlled in a manner that ensures easy retrieval and availability.

- Estimates of human error rates are based on a human reliability analysis of the data collection process to determine a reasonable rate of human error in MC&A data for the specific licensee.

- Reasonable estimates of human error rates include input regarding equipment design, plant policies and practices, and written procedures.

- Reasonable estimates of human error rates include input regarding situational and personnel factors that may produce errors.

- Any potential problems that can reasonably be resolved following a human reliability analysis are resolved and the estimates of a reasonable error rate recalculated.

Questions and Answers: Q   What minimum level of human error is reasonably achievable with respect to MC&A data?

A   The degree and amount of human error in MC&A data depends on the systems that are in place to provide checks and balances to reduce errors. An effective program to reduce human error would employ techniques that limit human error by reducing the chances for errors to be made and not creating error-likely situations in the design of the work. However, without totally eliminating the human element from MC&A, there is no way to eliminate human error totally. Table 1 lists some of the applicable human error rates and situational multipliers from Swain and Guttmann (1983).

Q Why should an independent observer be used to sign off on checklists and other work?

A An independent observer is useful in the event that a person makes a mistake, since an independent observer will often see mistakes whereas the person who made the original mistake, using the same logic or reviewing the work rather quickly, will be less likely to recognize the problem.

Table 1 Errors Rate Associated with MC&A Data Collection

These values are adapted from Swain and Guttmann (1983) and reflect some typical error probabilities for human activities in the MC&A process. For additional data and information on its usage, please refer to the cited document.

Potential Error	Estimated Error Rate
Failure to perform rule-based actions correctly when	
written procedures are available and used	0.005
written procedures are not available or used	1.0
Omitting a step or important instruction from	
a formal procedure	0.003
oral instructions	negligible
Writing an item incorrectly in response to	
a formal procedure	0.003
oral instructions	negligible
Carrying out a plant policy scheduled task such as periodic tests performed	
weekly, monthly, etc	0.01
Using a written test or calibration procedure properly	0.01
Using a checklist properly	0.5
Omitting items when procedures have check-off provisions and are	
correctly used	0.003
incorrectly used	0.01
Omitting items when written procedures are available and are	
not used	0.05
Errors of commission in reading and recording quantitative information from unannunciated displays	
analog meter	0.003
digital readout	0.001
chart recorder	0.006
printing recorder with large number of parameters	0.05
graphs	0.01
recording tasks	0.005
simple arithmetic calculation	0.01
Estimated probabilities that a checker will fail to detect errors made by others	
routine tasks, checker uses written materials	0.1
routine tasks, checker uses no written materials	0.2
one-of-a-kind checking with alerting factors	0.05
special measurements	0.01
Modifications of estimated error rates for the effects of stress and experience level	
low stress	x2
optimum stress	x1
moderately high	
stress novice	x4
skilled	x2
extremely high stress (life threatening)	
novice	x10
skilled	x5

4.10 Independent Assessment [§74.59(h)(4)]

Requirement

The rule requires that a licensee independently assess the past performance of the MC&A system and review its effectiveness at least once every 12 months, including management's action on prior assessment recommendations.

Intent and Scope

The intent of the independent assessment of the MC&A system is to periodically review the system performance from an effectiveness perspective relative to the performance objectives defined in §74.51(a) and the system capabilities defined in §74.51(b).

4.10.1 Assessment Program

Describe the structure of the program including:

- The means of assuring independence (from those responsible for MC&A functions) of action and objectivity of decision,

- The technical qualifications of and the selection criteria for team members,

- The planned objective and scope of the assessment, including a listing of the general areas to be covered, and

- The organizational positions responsible for initiating the assessment, approving the membership of the assessment team, implementing the corrective actions that are deemed necessary, and providing follow-up action to ensure that corrective actions have been satisfactorily implemented.

In the Annex, provide a checklist of the functions to be reviewed in each area. Regulatory Guide 5.51 may be used as appropriate.

Affirmations:

An effectiveness evaluation of the entire MC&A system is performed at least every 12 months.

The assessment is performed by technically qualified individuals whose organizational positions and normal work assignments will not interfere with their ability to make objective decisions.

The assessment team leader has no responsibility for performing or directly managing any part of the MC&A program.
The details and results of the assessments and recommended corrective actions are documented and reported to the plant manager within 30 days of completing all inspection, audit, surveillance, and interview activities associated with the total MC&A program assessment.

Management receives and evaluates the assessment report, documents its conclusions including any actions necessary to correct deficiencies identified in the assessment report, and issues the necessary directives to initiate such corrective actions. Management also documents its conclusions, including whether any action is to be taken, regarding recommendations made in the assessment report.

A tracking system is used to ensure that corrective actions are implemented.

The actions taken to correct deficiencies are documented and reviewed during the subsequent assessment.

Acceptance Criteria: The assessment includes a comprehensive review of the MC&A system to independently assess the system design and evaluate its capabilities to achieve the general safeguards objectives and an audit and inspection of the system performance, carried out in sufficient depth, to detect deficiencies or weaknesses in either the system design or implementation.

The assessment encompasses the entire MC&A system with particular emphasis on abrupt loss detection, item control, and alarm resolution. The emphasis is justified on the basis that these functions provide the primary assurance that no loss has occurred. The assessment program provides objective measures of:

- Management effectiveness and responsiveness to indications of possible loss,

- Staff training and qualifications for particular job functions,

- Quality control of measurements and process variability,

- Timeliness of loss detection and response to alarms, and

- Alarm resolution effectiveness.

The personnel assigned to the assessment team have an understanding of the objectives and requirements applicable to the MC&A system and have sufficient knowledge and experience to be able to assess the adequacy of the function they are requested to review. The team does not include MC&A management personnel but may include other MC&A staff provided no individual reviews his/her own area of responsibility nor the area of another MC&A team member.

The responsibility and authority for the assessment program and for initiating corrective actions are least one organizational level higher than the MC&A manager.

Outside contractor laboratories are included in the 12 month assessments.
When conducting a single total assessment, the assessment activities, other than final report writing, are completed within 30 calendar days of the initial team activities. If different elements of the MC&A program are assessed by different teams, the sub-assessments need not be conducted simultaneously, but all assessment activities (other than final report writing) across the total MC&A system are to be completed within a 90-day time span. When utilizing sub-assessments, each of the individual teams has the same team leader so as to assure an adequate integration of the individual sub-assessments, including a single final report.

4.11 SSNM Custodianship [§74.59(h)(5)]

Requirement

The rule requires that a licensee assign custodial responsibility for all SSNM possessed under licensee in a manner that ensures that such responsibility can be effectively executed.

Intent and Scope

The intent of this requirement is that there be a designated individual who is responsible for having knowledge of the placement and movement of SSNM within a specified area and transfers into and out of the area. Such an individual should be vested with the authority to obtain the information necessary to accomplish his/her task and to ensure that activities are carried out in accordance with approved policies and procedures.

4.11.1 Custodial Areas

Identify the areas into which the facility will be divided to ensure that custodianship can be effectively executed. Clarification can be provided by reference to facility drawings included in the Annex.

Affirmations:

The SSNM processing facility is subdivided into a sufficient number of areas to ensure that custodial responsibilities can be effectively executed.

Acceptance Criteria:

Except for the stipulations that all SSNM crossing custodial area boundaries must be measured and custodians must be able to effectively execute their duties, there are no restrictions on how large an area can be. However, different MAAs should have different custodians, and within MAA, areas with widely divergent functions should have different custodians. An example of the latter situation would be a fabrication plant where bulk material is handled in one area in the preparation of the fuel component of an element, and a second area is involved with machining and preparation of the element for higher tier fabrication.

4.11.2 Duties/Authority

Describe the duties of the SSNM custodians including defined authorities.

Affirmations:

A custodian and a minimum number of alternates are designated for each area subdivision.

SSNM transferred between areas of different custodial responsibility will have assigned values for element and fissile isotope based on measurements, which are certified on signed transfer documents.

Acceptance Criteria:

A current listing of designated custodians and alternates should be maintained.

Custodians should be familiar with SSNM processing activities as well as MC&A functions. A minimum of 1 year of experience in each of these areas is desirable.

Custodians should not be production or process operations personnel, so as to preclude the possibility of conflicts of interest.

REFERENCES

ANSI N15.36, *Non-Destructive Assay Measurement Control and Assurance*, American National Standards Institute, New York, New York, 1983.

ANSI N15.41, *Guide to Nuclear Facility Measurement Control*, American National Standards Institute, New York, New York, 1984.

R. H. Augustson, *DYMAC Demonstration Program: Phase I Experience*, LA-7126-MS, Los Alamos Scientific Laboratory, Los Alamos, New Mexico, 1978.

C. A. Bennett and M. Bowen, *Statistical Methods for Nuclear Material Management*, NUREG- 4604, U.S. Nuclear Regulatory Commission, Washington, D.C., 1988.

W. M. Bowen, *Evaluation of Simultaneous Testing Procedures for Nuclear Materials Control and Accounting*, NUREG/CR-2483 (PNL-4083), Pacific Northwest Laboratory, Richland, Washington, March 1982.

R. J. Brouns, and F. P. Roberts, *Training and Qualifying Personnel for Performing Measurements for the Control and Accounting of Special Nuclear Material* NUREG/CR-0773 (PNL-3020), Pacific Northwest Laboratory, Richland, Washington, November 1980.

R. J. Brouns, F. P. Roberts, J. A. Merrill, and W. B. Brown, *A Measurement Control Program for Nuclear Material Accounting*, NUREG/CR-0829 (PNL-3021), Pacific Northwest Laboratory, Richland, Washington, June 1980.

R. J. Brouns, B. W. Smith, D. W. Brite, and C. O. Harvey, *The Use of Process Monitoring Data for Nuclear Material Accounting: Vol. 1, Summary Report* NU CR-1670 (PNL-3396), Pacific Northwest Laboratory, Richland, Washington, 1980. (Available in abbreviated form as R. J. Brouns and B. W. Smith, "The Use of Process Monitoring Data to Enhance Material Accounting," In *Proceedings of the Institute of Nuclear Materials Management Meeting, IX*, pp. 688-696, Chicago, Illinois, 1980.)

D. D. Cobb, "Sequential Tests for Near-Real-Time Accounting," In *Proceedings of the Institute of Nuclear Materials Management Meeting, X*, pp.Z-70, Chicago, Illinois,

H. A. David, *Order Statistics*, John Wiley & Sons, New York, 1970.

R. F. Eggers, *Detailed Response to Alarms*, Technical Report to the NRC, Pacific Northwest Laboratory, Richland, Washington, 1981.

R. F. Eggers, *Design Aids for Estimating the Frequency of Occurrence of Unresolved Plant-Wide False Alarms*, Technical Report to the NRC, Pacific Northwest Laboratory, Richland, Washington, 1982.

C. Eisenhart, M. W. Hastay, and W. A. Wallis, *Selected Techniques of Statistical Analysis*, McGraw-Hill, New York, 1947.

J. E. Glancy, G. Borgonovi, S. Donelson et al., *Feasibility and Cost/Benefit of Advanced Safeguards for Control of Nuclear Material In-Process*, NUREG/ Vol. I (SAI 01580-343LJ), Science Applications, inc., a Jolla, California, October 1980.

F. A. Graybill, *Theory and Application of the Linear Model*, Duxbury Press. North Scituate, Massachusetts, 1976.

E. A. Hakkila, J. W. Barnes, T. R. Canada et al., *Coordinated Safeguards for Materials Management in a Fuel Reprocessing Plant*, Appendix (Part E), Vol. 11, Los Alamos Scientific Laboratory, Los Alamos, New Mexico, 1977.

E. A. Hakkila, D. D. Cobb, H. A. Dayem et al., *Materials Management in an Internationally Safeguarded Fuels Reprocessing-Plant*, LA-8042, Vols. 1, and 3, Los Alamos Scientific Laboratory, Los Alamos, New Mexico, 1980.

R. L. Hawkins, R. L. Lynch, and R. F. Lumb, *Using Advanced Process Monitoring to Improve Material Control*, NUREG/CR-1676, Vol. 1 (NUSAC-566), Nuclear Surveillance and Auditing Corporation, McLean, Virginia, 1980.

R. D. Hurt, S. J. Hurell, J. W. Wachter et al., *Experimental Demonstration of Microscopic Process Monitoring*, ORNL/TM-7848, Oak Ridge National Laboratory, Oak Ridge, Tennessee, 1982.

IAEA Safeguards Technical Manual, Part F - Statistical Concepts and Techniques, IAEA-174, International Atomic Energy Agency, Vienna, Austria, 1977.

J. L. Jaech, *Statistical Methods in Nuclear Material Control*, TID-26298, National Technical Information Service, Springfield, Virginia, 1973.

J. L. Jaech, "On Forming Linear Combinations of Accounting Data to Detect Constant Small Losses," *Journal of Nuclear Materials Management*, VI(4):37-42, 1977.

J. W. Johnston, R. R. Kinnison, J. S. Littlefield, and B. W. Smith, *Methods for Recurring Loss Test*, NUREG/CR-5002, U.S. Nuclear Regulatory Commission, Washington, D.C., 1987.

J. M. Juran, (ed.), *Quality Control Handbook*, McGraw-Hill Book Company, Inc., New York, New York, 1951.

Lumb and Associates, *Inventory Difference Evaluation Program (INDEP)*, 1986.

R. Lumb, and F. Tingey, *Mathematical Derivation of the Automated Material Accounting Statistics System (AMASS)*, Nuclear Surveillance and Auditing Corporation, McLean, Virginia, 1981.

J. T. Markin, A. L. Baker, and J. P. Shipley, "Implementing Advanced Data Analyses Techniques in Near-Real-Time Materials Accounting," in *Proceedings of the Institute of Nuclear Materials Management Meeting, IX*, pp. 3-244, Chicago, Illinois, 1980.

J. C. Miles, J. E. Glancy, and S. E. Donelson, *Use of Process Monitoring Data for the Enhancement of Nuclear Material Control and Accounting*, NUREG/CR-1013 (MLM-2643), Mound Laboratories, Miamisburg, Ohio, and Science Applications, Inc., La Jolla, California, 1979.

R. R. Picard, *NRCPAGE Applications Manual*, NUREG/CR-4497 (LA-10638-M), U.S. Nuclear Regulatory Commission, Washington, D.C., 1986.

P. T. Reardon, S. W. Heaberlin, and R. F. Eggers, "An Assessment Method to Predict the Rate of Unresolved False Alarms," In *Proceedings of the Institute of Nuclear Materials Management Meeting, XI*, pp. 278-282, Chicago, Illinois, 1982.

T. D. Reilly, N. Ensslin, H. Smith, and S. Kreiner, *Passive Nondestructive Assay of Nuclear Materials*, NUREG/CR-5550, U.S. Nuclear Regulatory Commission, Washington, D.C., 1991.

T. D. Reilly, and M. L. Evans, *Measurement Reliability for Nuclear Material Assay*, LA-6574, Los Alamos Scientific Laboratory, Los Alamos, New Mexico, 1977.

D. R. Rogers (ed.), *Handbook of Nuclear Safeguards Measurement Methods*, NUREG/CR-2078 (MLM-2855, Mound Laboratories, Miamisburg, Ohio, 1983.

D. M. Rose, and F. W. Scholz, *Statistical Analysis of Cumulative Shipper-Receiver Differences*, NUREG/CR-2819 (BCS 40384-0), Boeing Computer Services Company, Tukwilla, Washington, 1983.

C. R. Rudy, D. B. Armstrong, K. W. Foster, D. R. Rogers, and D. R. Hill, *Controlled Unit Approach: An Application Manual*, NUREG/CR-2538 (MLM-2881), Mound Facility, Miamisburg, Ohio, 1982.

P. W. Seabaugh, D. R. Rogers, H. A. Woltemann et al., *The Controllable Unit Approach to Material Control: Application to a High Throughput Mixed Oxide Process*; NUREG/CR-1214, Vol. 1 and Vol. 2 (MLM-2532), Mound Laboratories, Miamisburg, Ohio, 1980.

W. A. Shehart, *Economic Control of Quality of Manufactured Products*, D. Van Nostrand Co., New York, 1931.

J. P. Shipley, "Decision-Directed Materials Accounting Procedures: An Overview," In *Proceedings of the Institute of Nuclear Materials Management Meeting, X*, pp. 281-287, Chicago, Illinois, 1981.

B. W. Smith, *Development of MC&A Alarm Resolution Procedures*, NUREG/CR-4108, U.S. Nuclear Regulatory Commission, Washington, D.C., 1985.

B. W. Smith and J. Razvi, "Resolving MC&A Alarms from Process Monitoring in a Fuel Fabrication Facility," In *Proceeding of the Institute of Nuclear Materials Management Meeting, XIII*, pp. 302-329, Columbus, Ohio, 1984.

K. B. Stewart, "The Loss Detection Powers of Four Loss Estimators," *Journal of Nuclear Materials Management*, VII(3):74-80, 1978.

A. D. Swain, and H. E. Guttmann, *Handbook of Human Reliability Analysis with Emphasis on Nuclear Power Plant Applications*, NUREG/CR-1278, Sandia National Laboratories, Albuquerque, New Mexico, October 1983.

J. Tanner, *False Alarm Resolution Assessment Methodology*, Technical Report to the NRC, Pacific Northwest Laboratory, Richland, Washington, 1981.

F. H. Tingey, C. J. Barnhart, and R. F. Lumb, *Resolving the Components of Process Variability and Estimating the Uncertainty of the LEID*, NUSAC Report 752, Rev. 1, NUSAC, Inc., Reston, Virginia, 1983.

USNRC, NUREG/BR-0006, U.S. Nuclear Regulatory Commission, Washington, D.C.

M. A. Wincek, K. B. Stewart, and G. F. Piepel, *Statistical Methods for Evaluating Sequential Material Balance Data*, NUREG/CR-0683 (PNL-2920), Pacific Northwest Laboratory, Richland, Washington, 1979.

NRC FORM 335
(2-89)
NRCM 1102,
3201, 3202

U.S. NUCLEAR REGULATORY COMMISSION

BIBLIOGRAPHIC DATA SHEET

(See instructions on the reverse)

1. REPORT NUMBER (Assigned by NRC, Add Vol., Supp., Rev., and Addendum Numbers, If any.)
NUREG-1280 Rev. 1

2. TITLE AND SUBTITLE

Standard Format and Content Acceptance Criteria for the Material Control and Accounting (MC&A) Reform Amendment

3. DATE REPORT PUBLISHED

MONTH	YEAR
April	1995

4. FIN OR GRANT NUMBER

5. AUTHOR(S)

6. TYPE OF REPORT

7. PERIOD COVERED *(Inclusive Dates)*

8. PERFORMING ORGANIZATION — NAME AND ADDRESS *(If NRC, provide Division, Office or Region, U.S. Nuclear Regulatory Commission, and mailing address; if contractor, provide name and mailing address.)*

Division of Fuel Cycle Safety and Safeguards
Office of Nuclear Material Safety and Safeguards
U.S. Nuclear Regulatory Commission
Washington, DC 20555-0001

9. SPONSORING ORGANIZATION — NAME AND ADDRESS *(If NRC, type "Same as above"; if contractor, provide NRC Division, Office or Region, U.S. Nuclear Regulatory Commission, and mailing address.)*

Same as 8 above.

10. SUPPLEMENTARY NOTES

11. ABSTRACT *(200 words or less)*

In 1987 the NRC revised the material control and accounting requirements for NRC licensees authorized to possess and use a formula quantity(i.e., 5 formula kilograms or more) of strategic special nuclear material. Those revisions issued as 10CFR 47.51-59 require timely monitoring of in-process inventory and discrete items to detect anomalies potentially indicative of material losses. Timely detection and enhanced loss localization capabilities are beneficial to alarm resolution and also for material recovery in the event of an actual loss. NUREG-1280 was issued in 1987 to present criteria that could be used by applicants, licensees, and NRC license reviewers in the initial preparation and subsequent review of fundamental nuclear material control (FNMC) plans submitted in response to the Reform Amendment. This document is also intended for both licensees and license reviewers with respect to FNMC plan revisions. General performance objectives, system capabilities, process monitoring, item monitoring, alarm resolution, quality assurance, and accounting are addressed. This revision to NUREG-1280 is an expansion of the initial edition, which clarifies and expands upon several topics and addresses issues identified under Reform Amendment implementation experience.

12. KEY WORDS/DESCRIPTORS *(List words or phrases that will assist researchers in locating the report.)*

material control and accounting requirements, strategic special nuclear material, material losses, fundamental nuclear material control (FNMC)

13. AVAILABILITY STATEMENT

unlimited

14. SECURITY CLASSIFICATION

(This Page)

unclassified

(This Report)

unclassified

15. NUMBER OF PAGES

16. PRICE

NRC FORM 335 (2-89)

www.ingramcontent.com/pod-product-compliance
Lightning Source LLC
Chambersburg PA
CBHW080302290526
45790CB00005B/1904